THE UNITED STATES CONSTITUTION: A ROUND TABLE COMIC
IS AN ENTERTAINING WAY TO LEARN ABOUT THE FORMATION OF THE
UNITED STATES AND OUR COUNTRY'S FOUNDING FATHERS.
I'M LOOKING FORWARD TO SHARING IT WITH MY 9-YEAR OLD SON,
WHOSE NAME IS SAM ADAMS.

—TED ADAMS
CEO/PUBLISHER
IDW PUBLISHING

ROUND TABLE DOES IT AGAIN! THIS TIME THEY'VE OUTDONE
THEMSELVES AND CREATED A WONDERFUL, HISTORICALLY ACCURATE
DEPICTION OF THE U.S. CONSTITUTION AND THE HISTORY
SURROUNDING IT. THIS SHOULD BE READ ALONGSIDE TEXTBOOKS
AND IN SCHOOLS THROUGH OUT THE COUNTRY. HISTORY MADE FUN!
WHAT CAN BEAT THAT?!

—DAVID M. USLAN
PRODUCER & VP OF BUSINESS DEVELOPMENT
GRAPHICLY

SO MANY PEOPLE BELIEVE THAT COMICS ARE FOR KIDS OR FOLKS THAT
LIVE IN THEIR BASEMENT. BUT THEY FORGET THAT THE ART AND
STORYTELLING OF THE FORMAT CAN TAKE SOMETHING AS DRY AS THE
                                        E IN A WAY THAT A CRUSTY
                                        ULD. ROUND TABLE'S
                                        TITUTION IS THE TYPE OF
                                        JIRED READING BY ALL.

                                        OWIN
                                    COMMUNITY CARETAKER

The United States Constitution: A Round Table Comic

© 2012 Writers of the Round Table Press

Round Table Comics
www.RoundTableCompanies.com
www.RoundTableComics.com

Round Table Companies
1670 Valencia Way
Mundelein, Il 60060, Usa
Phone: 815-346-2398

Publisher: Corey Michael Blake
Executive Editor, Digital Distribution: David C. Cohen
Illustration/Coloring, Front Cover: Nathan Lueth
Interior Design/Layout, Back Cover: Sunny DiMartino
Proofreading: Rita Hess

Printed In Canada

First Edition: Feb 2012
10 9 8 7 6 5 4 3 2 1

Library Of Congress Cataloging-In-Publication Data
The United States Constitution: A Round Table Comic /
Writers of the Round Table Press.—1st ed. p. cm.
ISBN: 978-1-6106-6025-9
Library of Congress Control Number: 2012931904
1. U.S. History. 2. Education. I. Title.

THE UNITED STATES
CONSTITUTION

A Round Table Comic

Writers of the Round Table Press

rtc
ROUND TABLE
COMICS

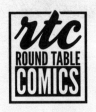

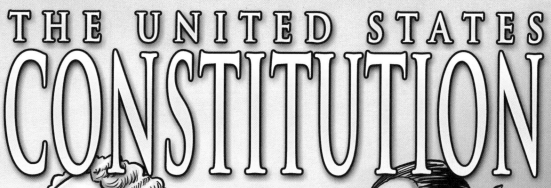

THE UNITED STATES CONSTITUTION

A Round Table Comic

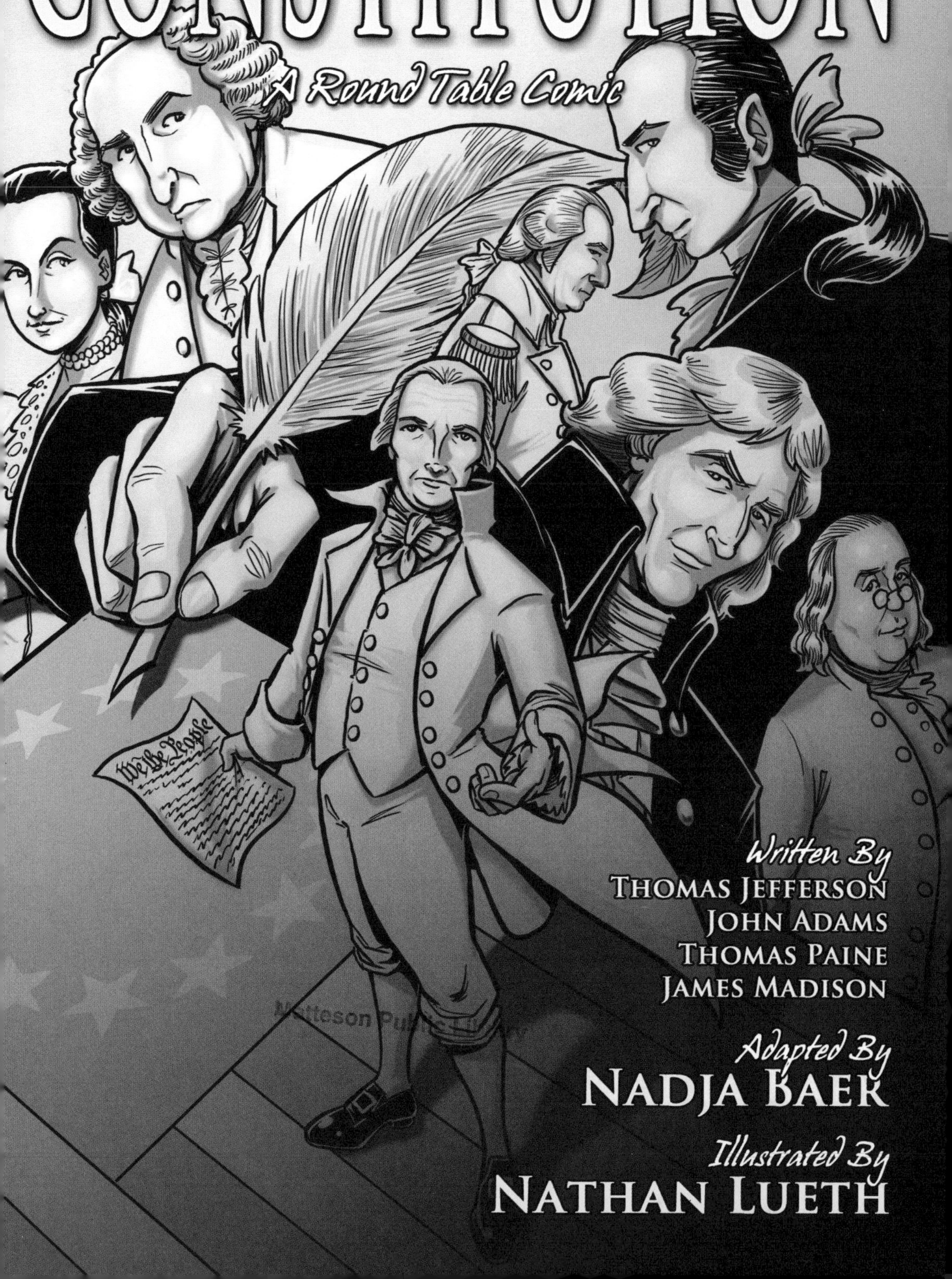

We the People

Written By
THOMAS JEFFERSON
JOHN ADAMS
THOMAS PAINE
JAMES MADISON

Adapted By
NADJA BAEK

Illustrated By
NATHAN LUETH

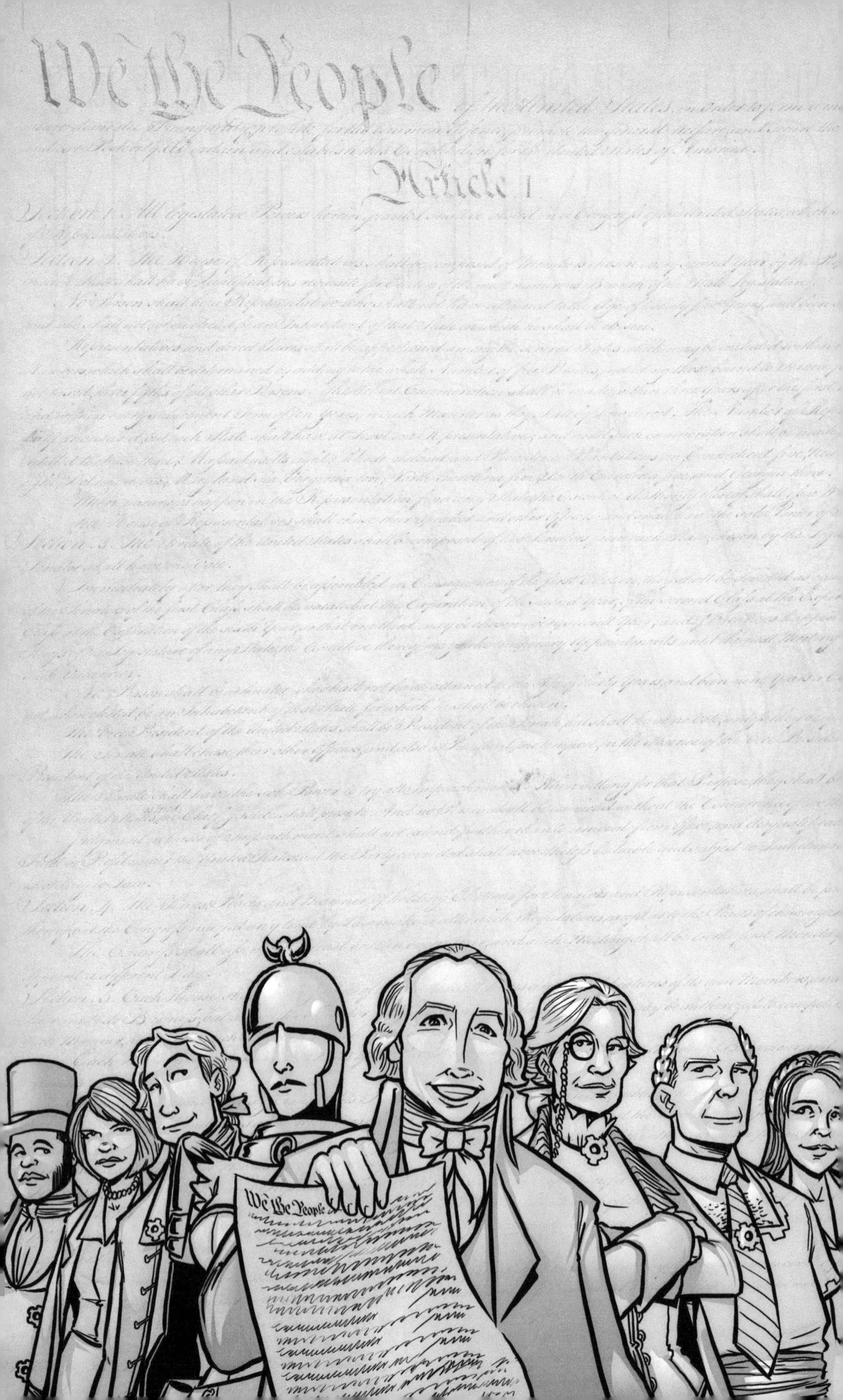

We the People
Article I
We the People

INTRODUCTION

THE UNITED STATES CONSTITUTION IS ONE OF THE MOST IMPORTANT DOCUMENTS IN OUR COUNTRY'S HISTORY, BUT THAT DOESN'T MEAN IT'S AN EASY READ. EVERY YEAR, MILLIONS OF STUDENTS AND HOPEFUL NEW CITIZENS ACROSS THE COUNTRY MEMORIZE THE PREAMBLE AND THE SYSTEM OF CHECKS AND BALANCES, BUT NOT MANY ARE ABLE TO SIFT THROUGH THE ARCHAIC LANGUAGE AND RETAIN MORE THAN THE BASIC FACTS. ONCE THE EXAM IS PASSED, HOW MANY STOP TO THINK ABOUT WHAT THE WORDS MEANT IN 1787 OR WHAT THEY MEAN TODAY?

THE UNITED STATES CONSTITUTION: A ROUND TABLE COMIC PRESENTS THE ENTIRE CONTENT OF THE ORIGINAL DOCUMENT AND A BEHIND-THE-SCENES LOOK AT SOME OF THE DEBATES THAT ITS CREATORS WENT THROUGH TO ACHIEVE A BALANCED SYSTEM OF POLITICAL POWER. THE HOT PHILADELPHIA SUMMER COMES ALIVE THROUGH THEIR CONSTANT ARGUMENTS AND THE COMPROMISES THEY REACHED IN THE STRUGGLE TO SECURE RATIFICATION. BY OFFERING A MIXTURE OF ENGAGING NARRATIVE, VISUALS, AND HISTORICAL TEXT, THIS GRAPHIC ADAPTATION INTRODUCES OUR FOREFATHERS AS UNIQUE PERSONALITIES AND HIGHLIGHTS THE RIGHTS AND FREEDOMS THEY FOUGHT TO SECURE FOR THEMSELVES AND FOR THE FUTURE OF THE NATION.

AT ROUND TABLE COMPANIES, WE ARE EXCITED TO BRING TO YOU A GRAPHIC NOVEL THAT WILL ENHANCE LEARNING ABOUT THIS IMPORTANT PIECE OF OUR COLLECTIVE HISTORY. THE MEN WHO WROTE THE DOCUMENT KEPT FUTURE GENERATIONS IN MIND THROUGHOUT THE WRITING PROCESS; IT IS FITTING THAT WE ARE ABLE TO UNDERSTAND WHAT THEY WENT THROUGH WHEN WE READ IT. WITH SO MANY CURRENT POLITICAL DEBATES AND LAWS BEING MOLDED AROUND THIS FRAMEWORK, WE FEEL THAT *THE UNITED STATES CONSTITUTION: A ROUND TABLE COMIC* PRESENTS AN EXCELLENT OPPORTUNITY TO EDUCATE READERS THROUGH AN ENTERTAINING AND RELATIVELY UNEXPLORED MEDIUM.

—THE ROUND TABLE COMPANIES FAMILY

WWW.ROUNDTABLECOMICS.COM

FOR MORE INFORMATION ABOUT THE FREE
CURRICULUM FOR EDUCATORS DEVELOPED BY MAUPIN
HOUSE AND DR. KATIE MONNIN, PROFESSOR OF
LITERACY AT THE UNIVERSITY OF NORTH FLORIDA,
PLEASE SEE THE BACK OF THE BOOK.

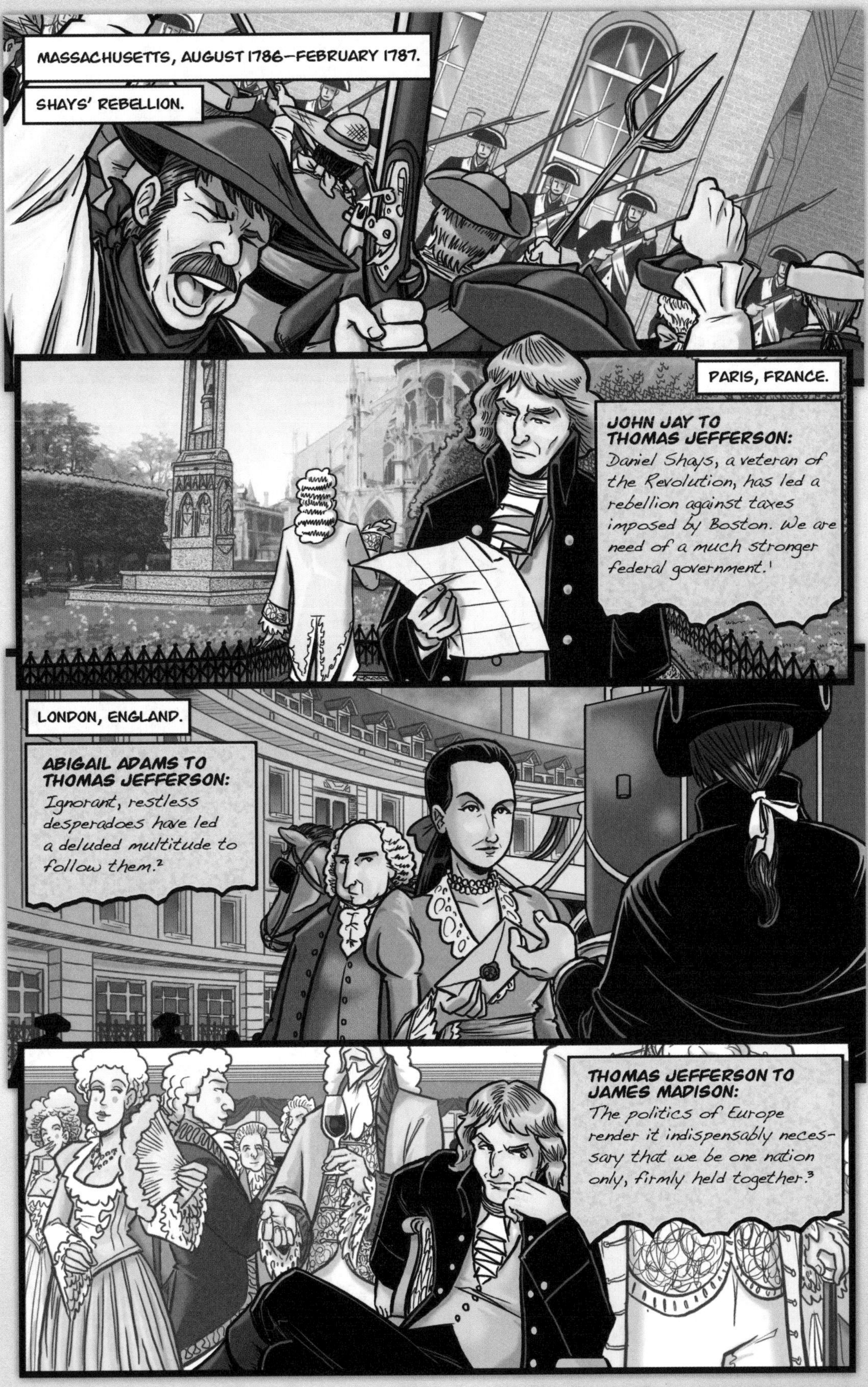
MASSACHUSETTS, AUGUST 1786—FEBRUARY 1787.
SHAYS' REBELLION.
PARIS, FRANCE.
JOHN JAY TO THOMAS JEFFERSON:
Daniel Shays, a veteran of the Revolution, has led a rebellion against taxes imposed by Boston. We are need of a much stronger federal government.[1]
LONDON, ENGLAND.
ABIGAIL ADAMS TO THOMAS JEFFERSON:
Ignorant, restless desperadoes have led a deluded multitude to follow them.[2]
THOMAS JEFFERSON TO JAMES MADISON:
The politics of Europe render it indispensably neces-sary that we be one nation only, firmly held together.[3]

[1] JOSEPH ELLIS, AMERICAN SPHINX (NEW YORK: VINTAGE BOOKS, 1998), 117. [2] ELLIS, 117. [3] ELLIS, 116.

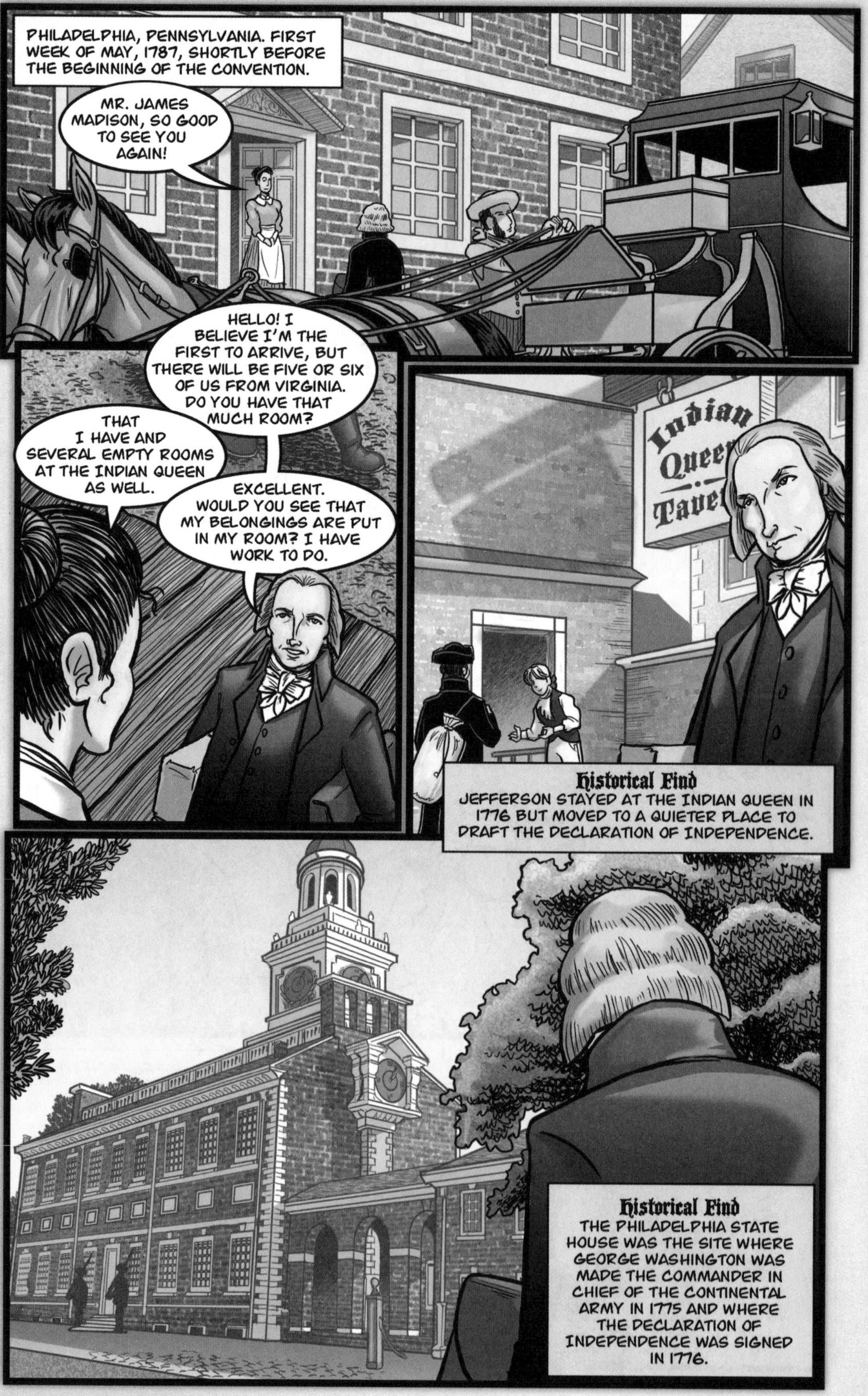
PHILADELPHIA, PENNSYLVANIA. FIRST WEEK OF MAY, 1787, SHORTLY BEFORE THE BEGINNING OF THE CONVENTION.
MR. JAMES MADISON, SO GOOD TO SEE YOU AGAIN!
HELLO! I BELIEVE I'M THE FIRST TO ARRIVE, BUT THERE WILL BE FIVE OR SIX OF US FROM VIRGINIA. DO YOU HAVE THAT MUCH ROOM?
THAT I HAVE AND SEVERAL EMPTY ROOMS AT THE INDIAN QUEEN AS WELL.
EXCELLENT. WOULD YOU SEE THAT MY BELONGINGS ARE PUT IN MY ROOM? I HAVE WORK TO DO.
Historical Find
JEFFERSON STAYED AT THE INDIAN QUEEN IN 1776 BUT MOVED TO A QUIETER PLACE TO DRAFT THE DECLARATION OF INDEPENDENCE.
Historical Find
THE PHILADELPHIA STATE HOUSE WAS THE SITE WHERE GEORGE WASHINGTON WAS MADE THE COMMANDER IN CHIEF OF THE CONTINENTAL ARMY IN 1775 AND WHERE THE DECLARATION OF INDEPENDENCE WAS SIGNED IN 1776.

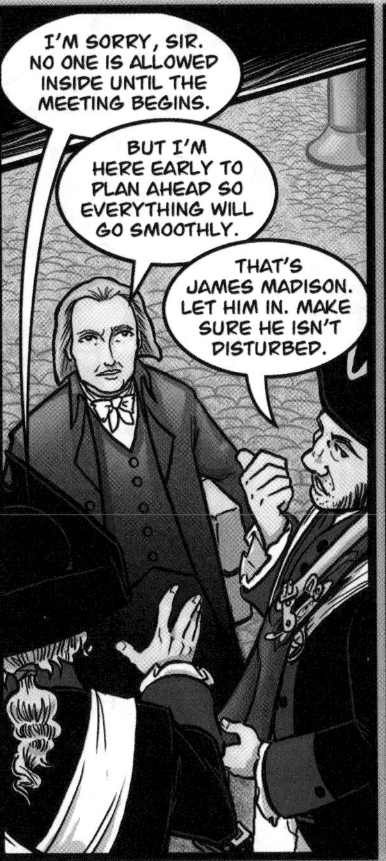
I'M SORRY, SIR. NO ONE IS ALLOWED INSIDE UNTIL THE MEETING BEGINS.
BUT I'M HERE EARLY TO PLAN AHEAD SO EVERYTHING WILL GO SMOOTHLY.
THAT'S JAMES MADISON. LET HIM IN. MAKE SURE HE ISN'T DISTURBED.

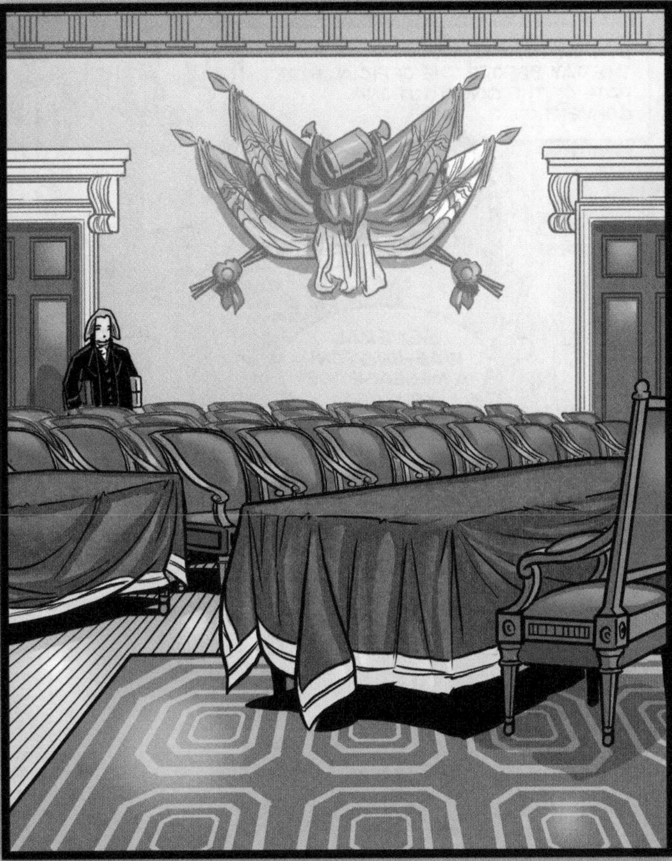

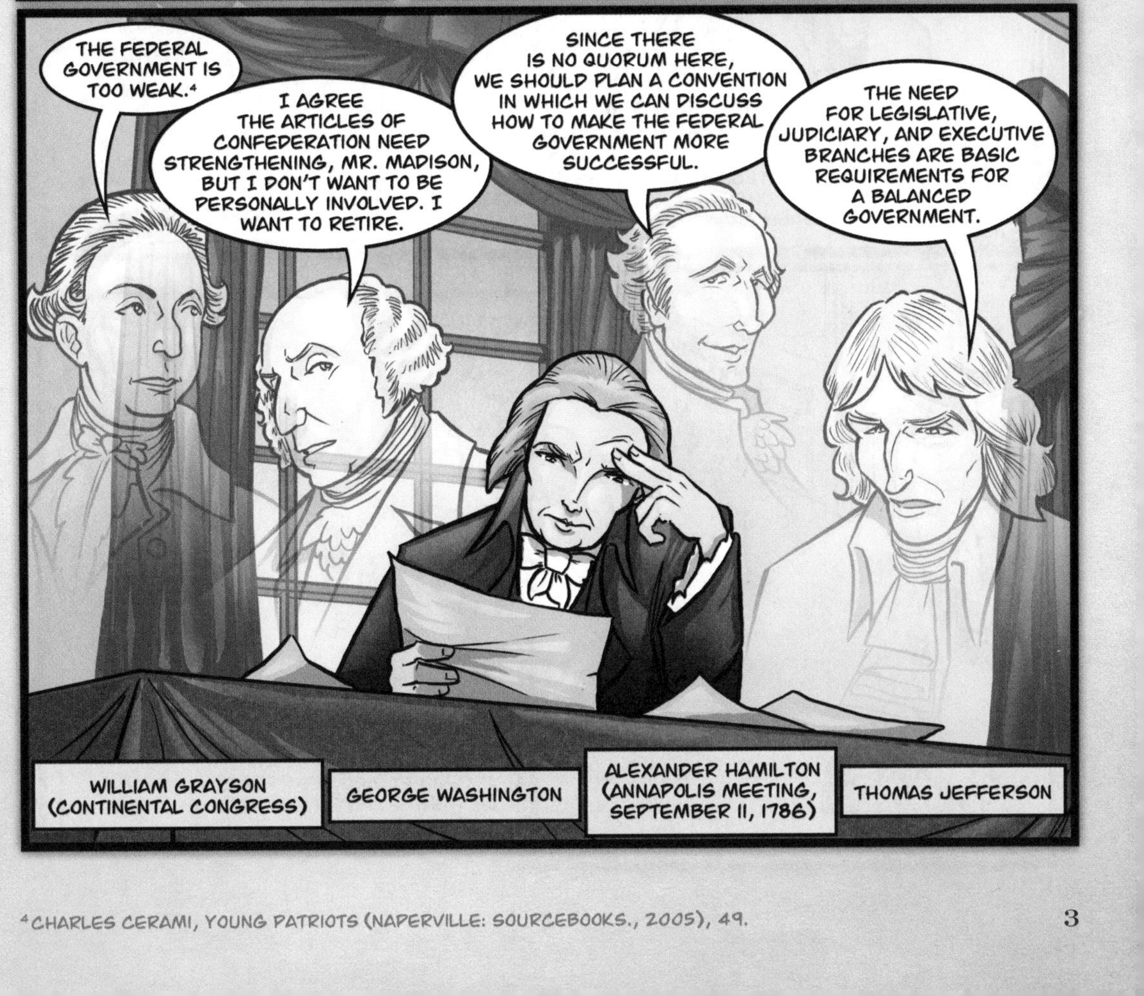
THE FEDERAL GOVERNMENT IS TOO WEAK.[4]
I AGREE THE ARTICLES OF CONFEDERATION NEED STRENGTHENING, MR. MADISON, BUT I DON'T WANT TO BE PERSONALLY INVOLVED. I WANT TO RETIRE.
SINCE THERE IS NO QUORUM HERE, WE SHOULD PLAN A CONVENTION IN WHICH WE CAN DISCUSS HOW TO MAKE THE FEDERAL GOVERNMENT MORE SUCCESSFUL.
THE NEED FOR LEGISLATIVE, JUDICIARY, AND EXECUTIVE BRANCHES ARE BASIC REQUIREMENTS FOR A BALANCED GOVERNMENT.
WILLIAM GRAYSON (CONTINENTAL CONGRESS)
GEORGE WASHINGTON
ALEXANDER HAMILTON (ANNAPOLIS MEETING, SEPTEMBER 11, 1786)
THOMAS JEFFERSON

[4] CHARLES CERAMI, YOUNG PATRIOTS (NAPERVILLE: SOURCEBOOKS., 2005), 49.

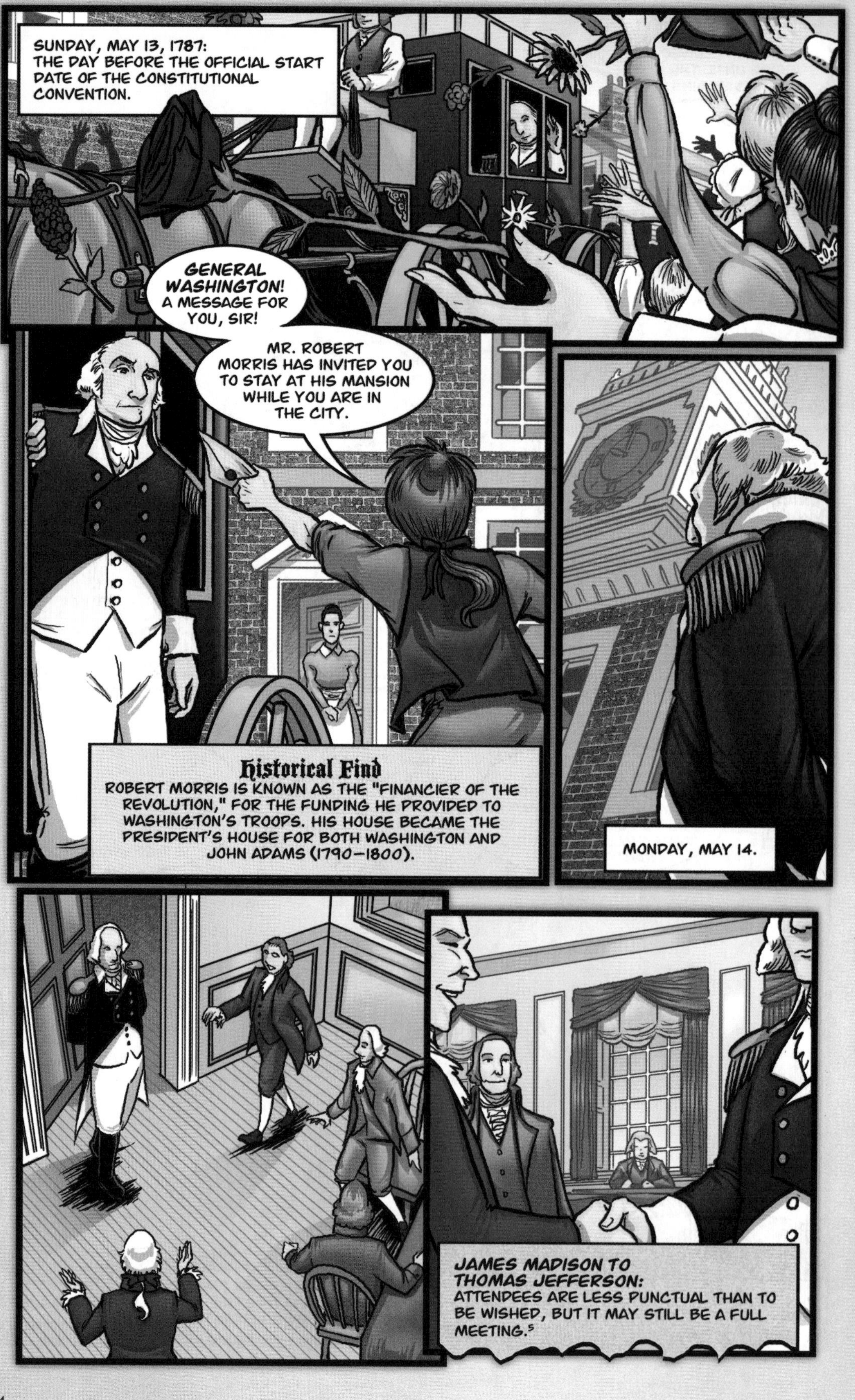
SUNDAY, MAY 13, 1787: THE DAY BEFORE THE OFFICIAL START DATE OF THE CONSTITUTIONAL CONVENTION.
GENERAL WASHINGTON! A MESSAGE FOR YOU, SIR!
MR. ROBERT MORRIS HAS INVITED YOU TO STAY AT HIS MANSION WHILE YOU ARE IN THE CITY.
Historical Find
ROBERT MORRIS IS KNOWN AS THE "FINANCIER OF THE REVOLUTION," FOR THE FUNDING HE PROVIDED TO WASHINGTON'S TROOPS. HIS HOUSE BECAME THE PRESIDENT'S HOUSE FOR BOTH WASHINGTON AND JOHN ADAMS (1790–1800).
MONDAY, MAY 14.
JAMES MADISON TO THOMAS JEFFERSON:
ATTENDEES ARE LESS PUNCTUAL THAN TO BE WISHED, BUT IT MAY STILL BE A FULL MEETING.[5]

[5] CERAMI, 103–104.

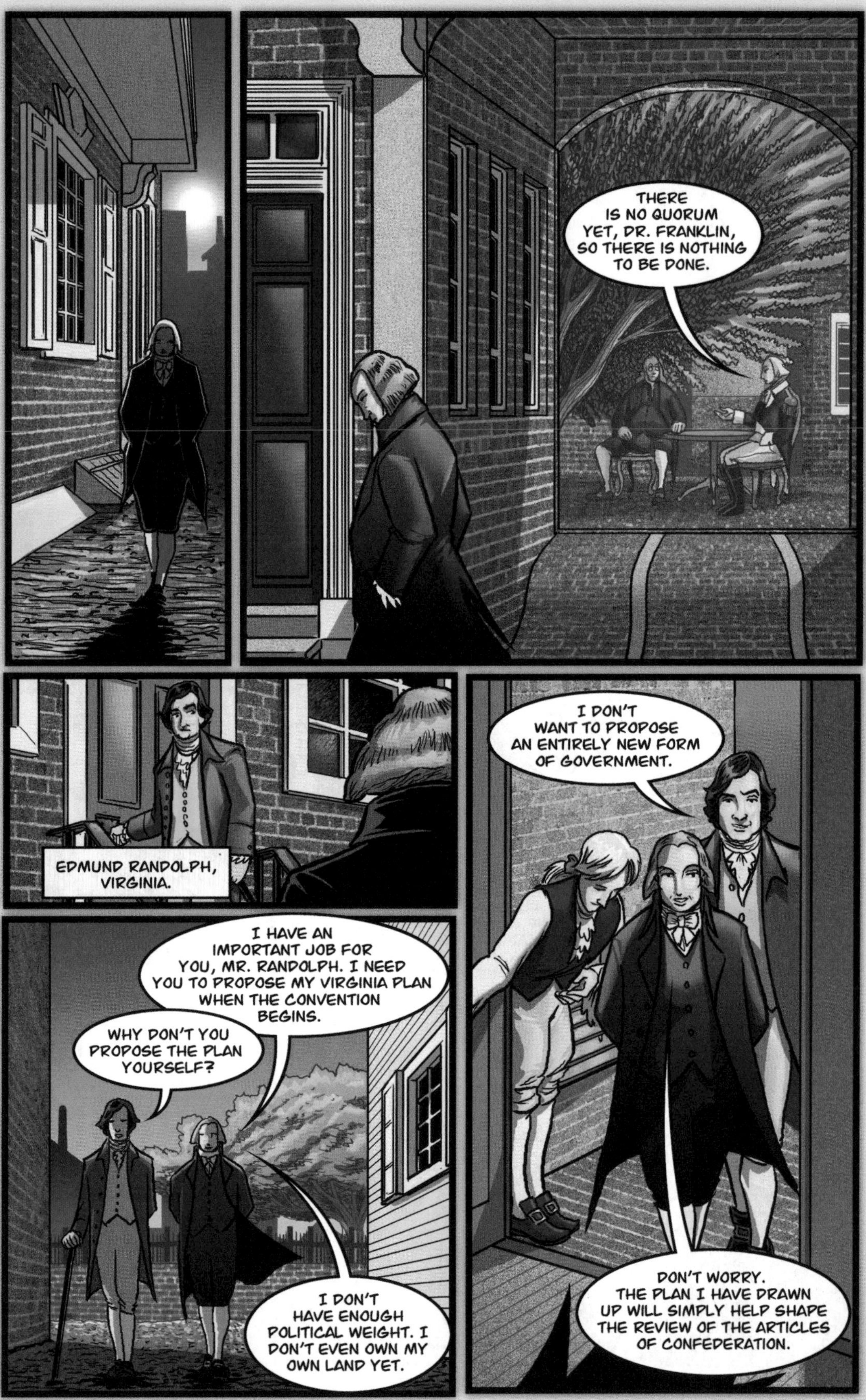
THERE IS NO QUORUM YET, DR. FRANKLIN, SO THERE IS NOTHING TO BE DONE.
EDMUND RANDOLPH, VIRGINIA.
I DON'T WANT TO PROPOSE AN ENTIRELY NEW FORM OF GOVERNMENT.
I HAVE AN IMPORTANT JOB FOR YOU, MR. RANDOLPH. I NEED YOU TO PROPOSE MY VIRGINIA PLAN WHEN THE CONVENTION BEGINS.
WHY DON'T YOU PROPOSE THE PLAN YOURSELF?
I DON'T HAVE ENOUGH POLITICAL WEIGHT. I DON'T EVEN OWN MY OWN LAND YET.
DON'T WORRY. THE PLAN I HAVE DRAWN UP WILL SIMPLY HELP SHAPE THE REVIEW OF THE ARTICLES OF CONFEDERATION.

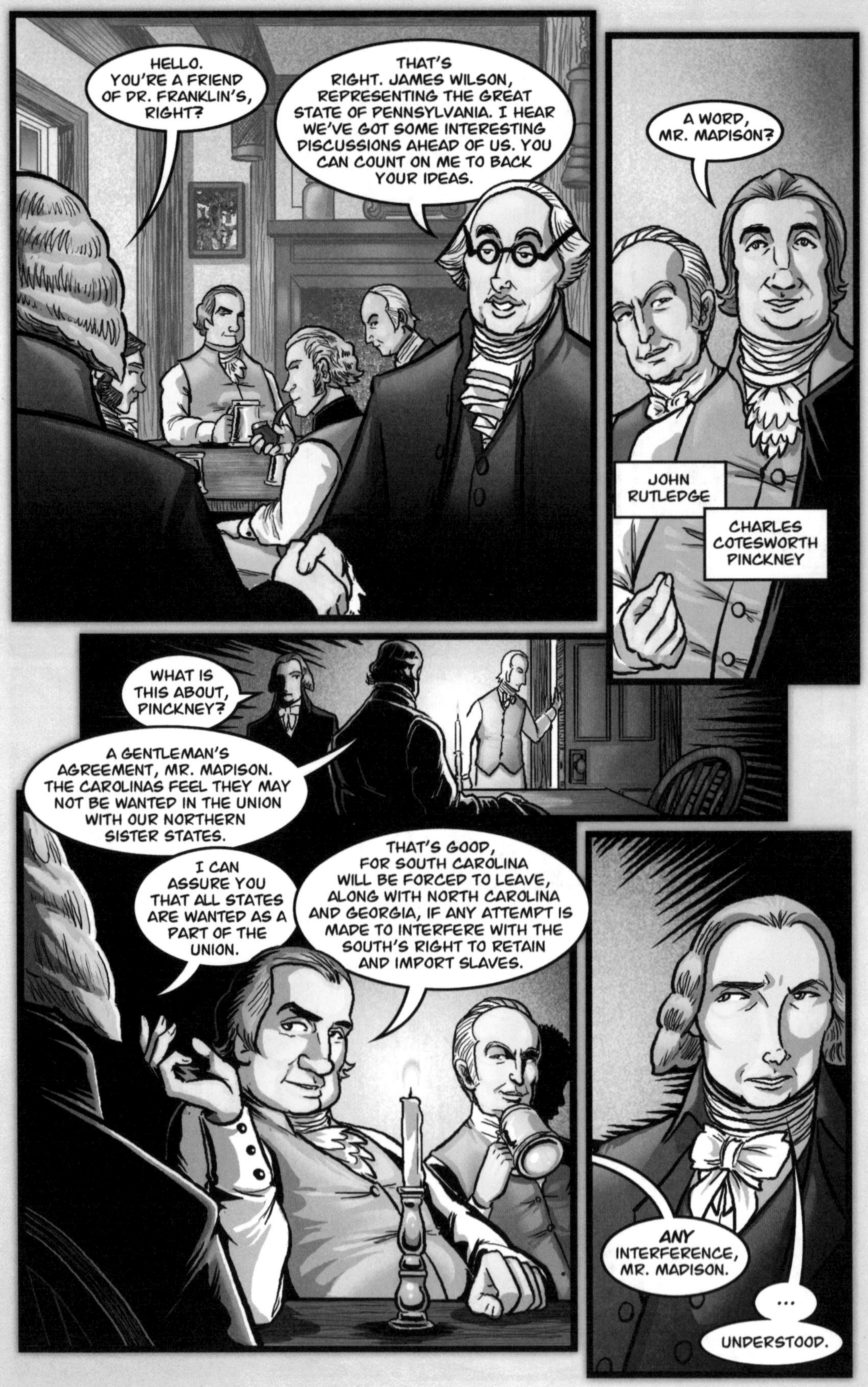
HELLO. YOU'RE A FRIEND OF DR. FRANKLIN'S, RIGHT?
THAT'S RIGHT. JAMES WILSON, REPRESENTING THE GREAT STATE OF PENNSYLVANIA. I HEAR WE'VE GOT SOME INTERESTING DISCUSSIONS AHEAD OF US. YOU CAN COUNT ON ME TO BACK YOUR IDEAS.
A WORD, MR. MADISON?
JOHN RUTLEDGE
CHARLES COTESWORTH PINCKNEY
WHAT IS THIS ABOUT, PINCKNEY?
A GENTLEMAN'S AGREEMENT, MR. MADISON. THE CAROLINAS FEEL THEY MAY NOT BE WANTED IN THE UNION WITH OUR NORTHERN SISTER STATES.
I CAN ASSURE YOU THAT ALL STATES ARE WANTED AS A PART OF THE UNION.
THAT'S GOOD, FOR SOUTH CAROLINA WILL BE FORCED TO LEAVE, ALONG WITH NORTH CAROLINA AND GEORGIA, IF ANY ATTEMPT IS MADE TO INTERFERE WITH THE SOUTH'S RIGHT TO RETAIN AND IMPORT SLAVES.
ANY INTERFERENCE, MR. MADISON.
...
UNDERSTOOD.

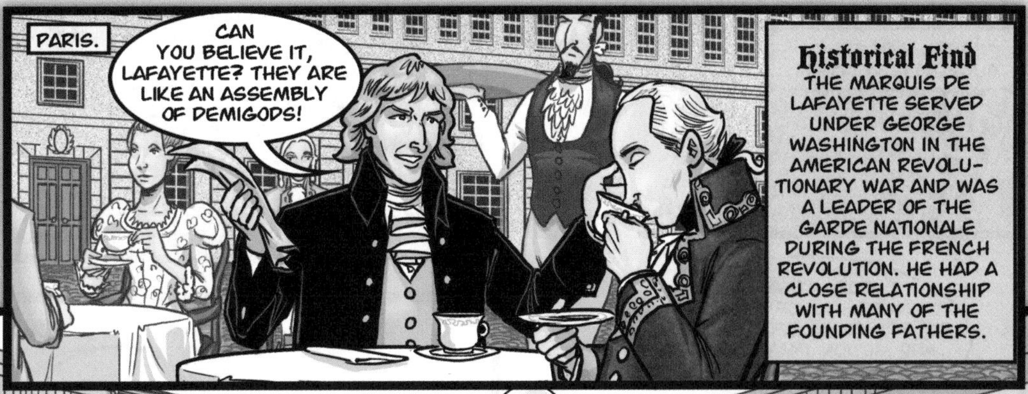
PARIS.
CAN YOU BELIEVE IT, LAFAYETTE? THEY ARE LIKE AN ASSEMBLY OF DEMIGODS!
Historical Find
THE MARQUIS DE LAFAYETTE SERVED UNDER GEORGE WASHINGTON IN THE AMERICAN REVOLUTIONARY WAR AND WAS A LEADER OF THE GARDE NATIONALE DURING THE FRENCH REVOLUTION. HE HAD A CLOSE RELATIONSHIP WITH MANY OF THE FOUNDING FATHERS.

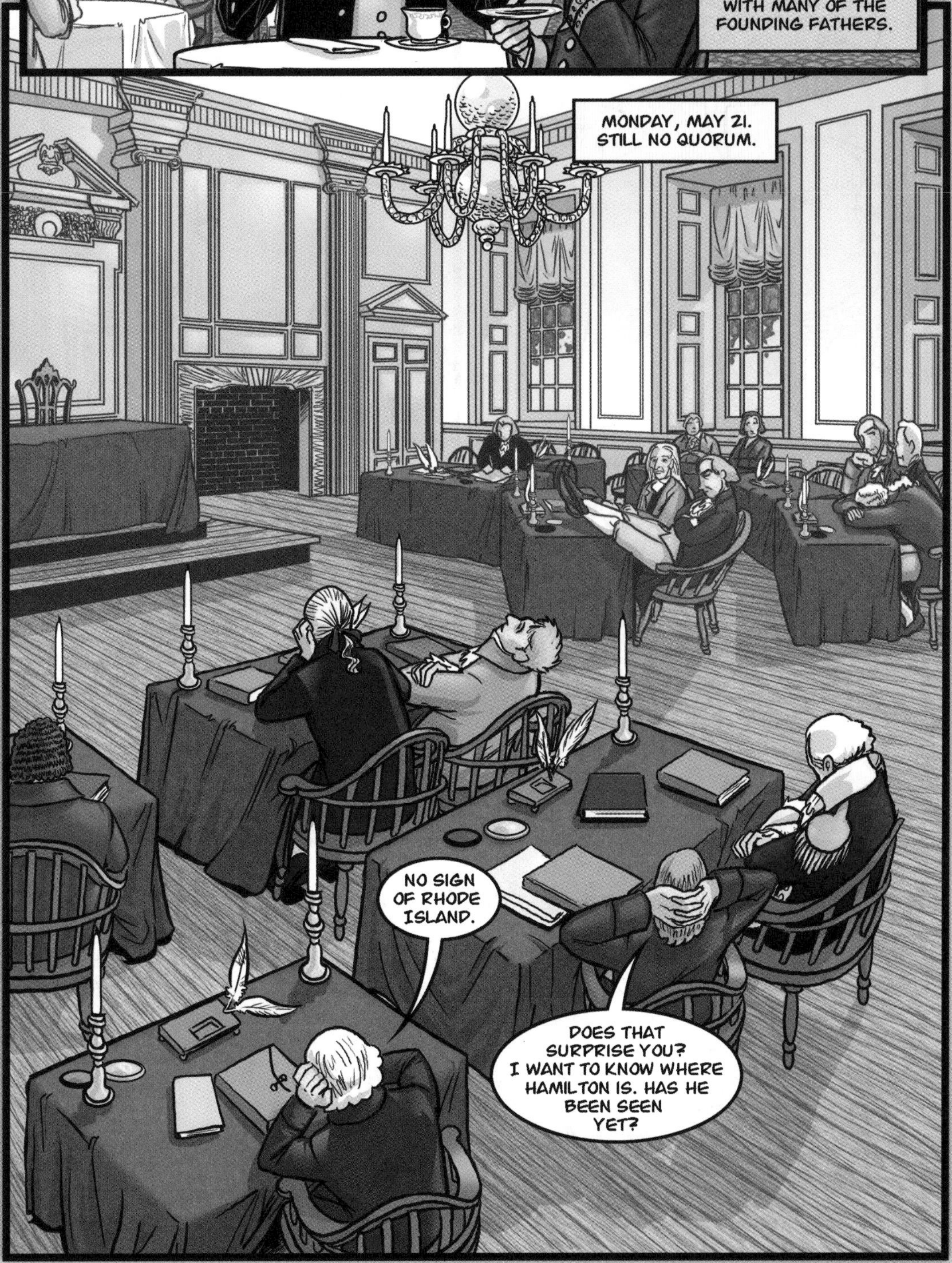
MONDAY, MAY 21. STILL NO QUORUM.
NO SIGN OF RHODE ISLAND.
DOES THAT SURPRISE YOU? I WANT TO KNOW WHERE HAMILTON IS. HAS HE BEEN SEEN YET?

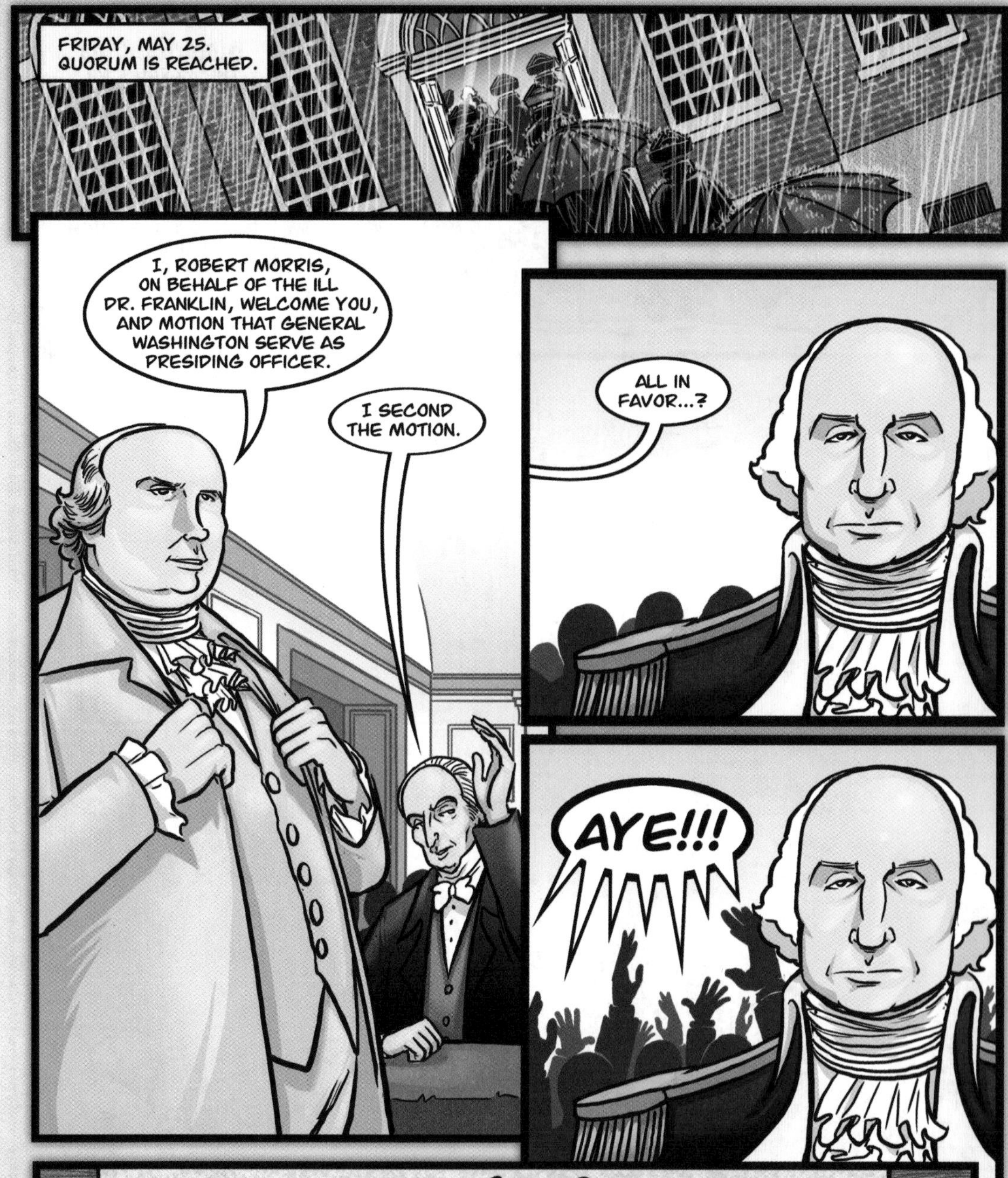
FRIDAY, MAY 25.
QUORUM IS REACHED.
I, ROBERT MORRIS, ON BEHALF OF THE ILL DR. FRANKLIN, WELCOME YOU, AND MOTION THAT GENERAL WASHINGTON SERVE AS PRESIDING OFFICER.
I SECOND THE MOTION.
ALL IN FAVOR...?
AYE!!!

Ground rules for the Convention:

-Votes will be recorded in geographical order from New Hampshire to Georgia and cast by state.
-Do not interrupt or cross in front of others when they have the floor.
-Arguing about the institution of slavery will not benefit our cause.
-Nothing spoken in house shall be printed or published without leave. Neither the notes taken by the secretary nor James Madison's detailed journal of events will be made public before 50 years have passed.

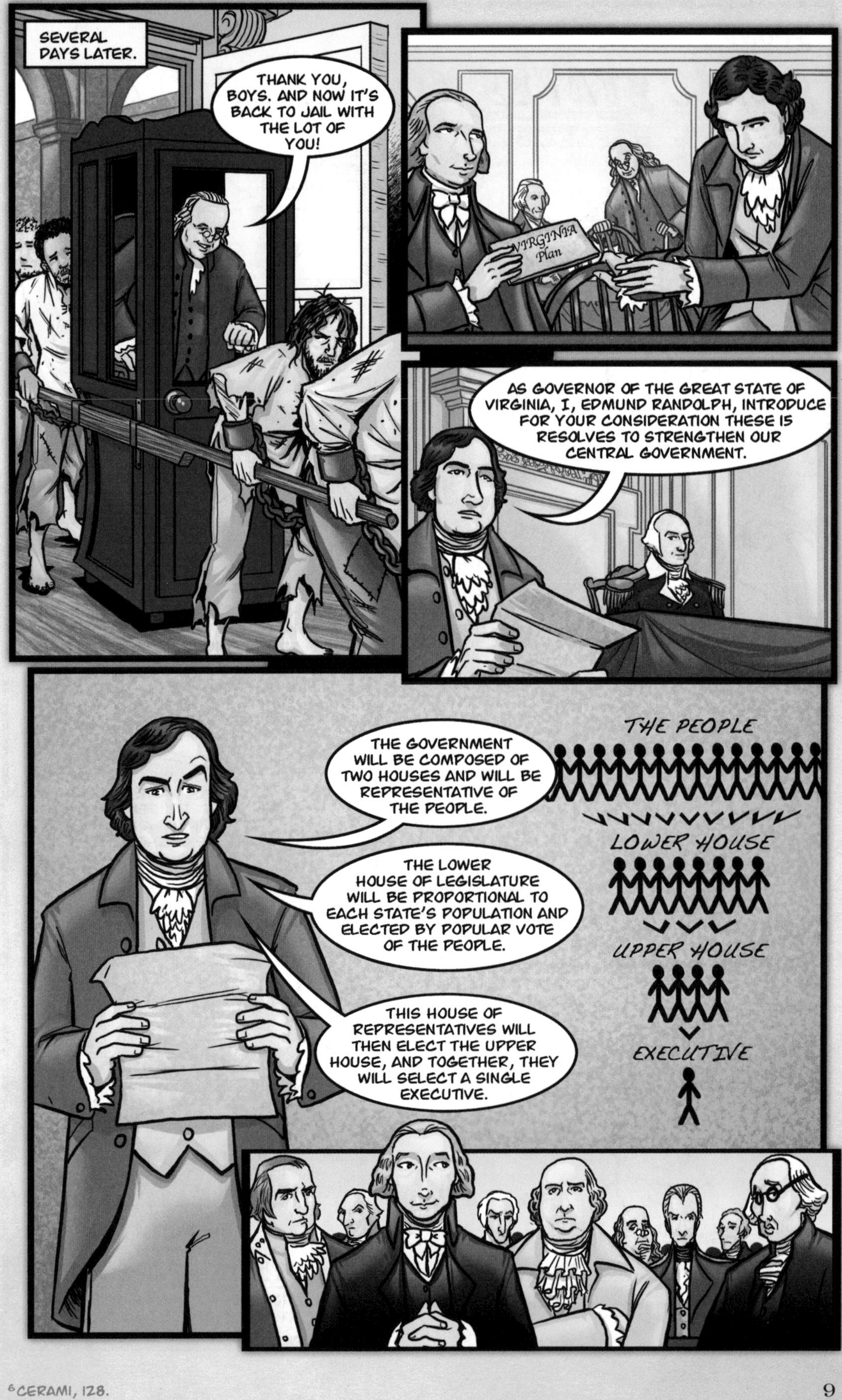
SEVERAL DAYS LATER.
THANK YOU, BOYS. AND NOW IT'S BACK TO JAIL WITH THE LOT OF YOU!
VIRGINIA Plan
AS GOVERNOR OF THE GREAT STATE OF VIRGINIA, I, EDMUND RANDOLPH, INTRODUCE FOR YOUR CONSIDERATION THESE 15 RESOLVES TO STRENGTHEN OUR CENTRAL GOVERNMENT.
THE GOVERNMENT WILL BE COMPOSED OF TWO HOUSES AND WILL BE REPRESENTATIVE OF THE PEOPLE.
THE LOWER HOUSE OF LEGISLATURE WILL BE PROPORTIONAL TO EACH STATE'S POPULATION AND ELECTED BY POPULAR VOTE OF THE PEOPLE.
THIS HOUSE OF REPRESENTATIVES WILL THEN ELECT THE UPPER HOUSE, AND TOGETHER, THEY WILL SELECT A SINGLE EXECUTIVE.
THE PEOPLE
LOWER HOUSE
UPPER HOUSE
EXECUTIVE

[6] CERAMI, 128.

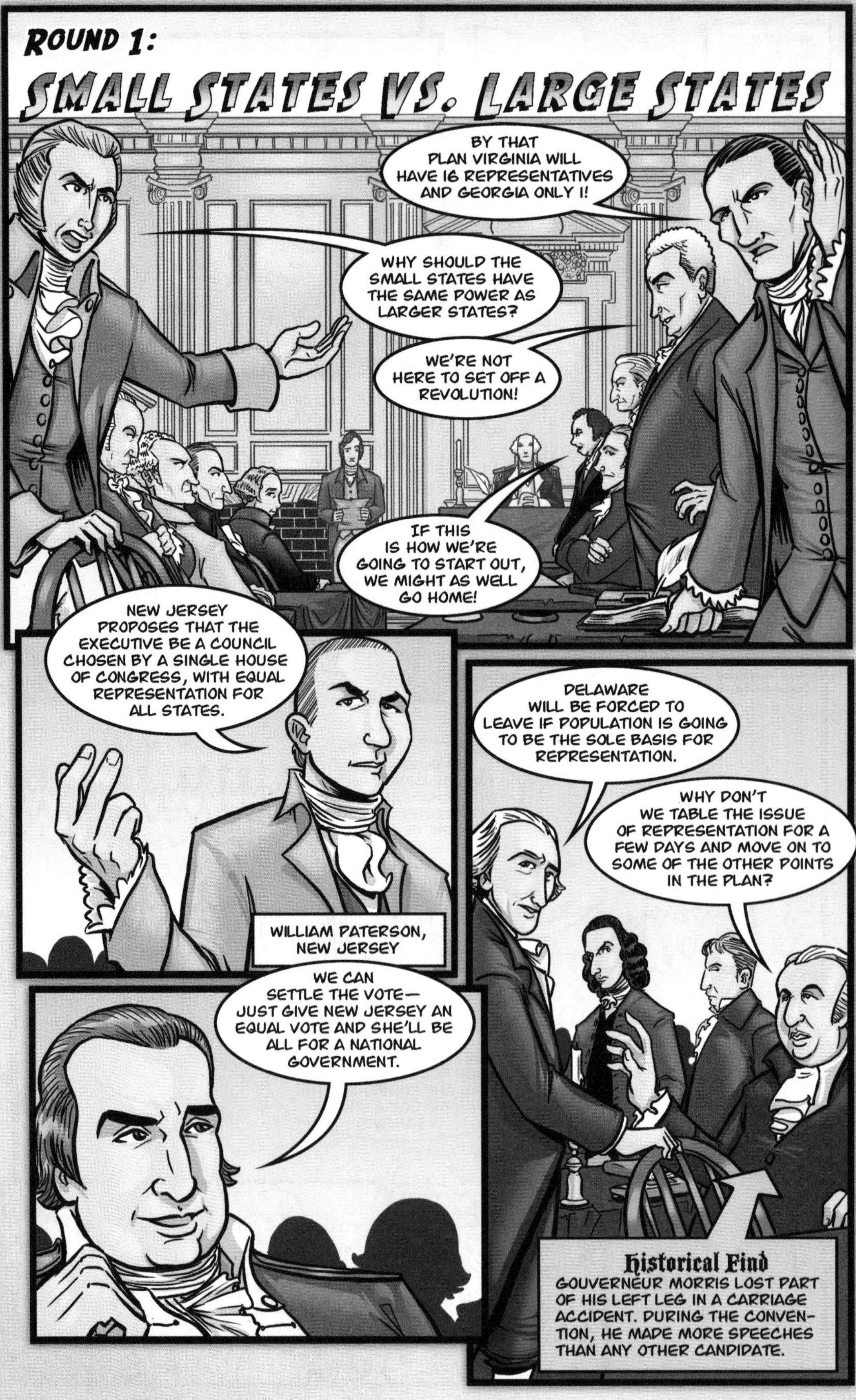
ROUND 1:
SMALL STATES VS. LARGE STATES
BY THAT PLAN VIRGINIA WILL HAVE 16 REPRESENTATIVES AND GEORGIA ONLY 1!
WHY SHOULD THE SMALL STATES HAVE THE SAME POWER AS LARGER STATES?
WE'RE NOT HERE TO SET OFF A REVOLUTION!
IF THIS IS HOW WE'RE GOING TO START OUT, WE MIGHT AS WELL GO HOME!
NEW JERSEY PROPOSES THAT THE EXECUTIVE BE A COUNCIL CHOSEN BY A SINGLE HOUSE OF CONGRESS, WITH EQUAL REPRESENTATION FOR ALL STATES.
WILLIAM PATERSON, NEW JERSEY
WE CAN SETTLE THE VOTE—JUST GIVE NEW JERSEY AN EQUAL VOTE AND SHE'LL BE ALL FOR A NATIONAL GOVERNMENT.
DELAWARE WILL BE FORCED TO LEAVE IF POPULATION IS GOING TO BE THE SOLE BASIS FOR REPRESENTATION.
WHY DON'T WE TABLE THE ISSUE OF REPRESENTATION FOR A FEW DAYS AND MOVE ON TO SOME OF THE OTHER POINTS IN THE PLAN?
Historical Find
GOUVERNEUR MORRIS LOST PART OF HIS LEFT LEG IN A CARRIAGE ACCIDENT. DURING THE CONVENTION, HE MADE MORE SPEECHES THAN ANY OTHER CANDIDATE.

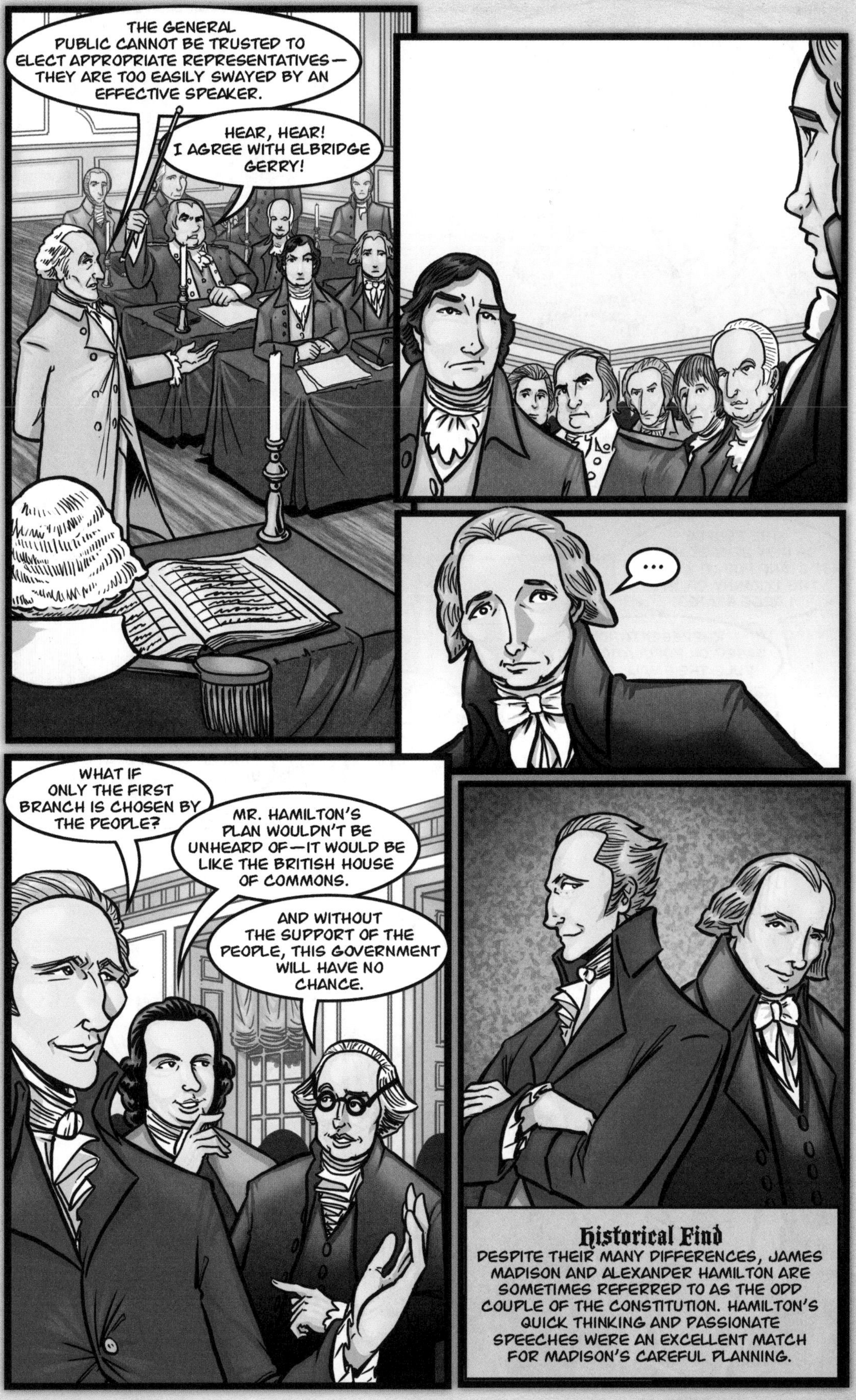
THE GENERAL PUBLIC CANNOT BE TRUSTED TO ELECT APPROPRIATE REPRESENTATIVES—THEY ARE TOO EASILY SWAYED BY AN EFFECTIVE SPEAKER.
HEAR, HEAR! I AGREE WITH ELBRIDGE GERRY!
...
WHAT IF ONLY THE FIRST BRANCH IS CHOSEN BY THE PEOPLE?
MR. HAMILTON'S PLAN WOULDN'T BE UNHEARD OF—IT WOULD BE LIKE THE BRITISH HOUSE OF COMMONS.
AND WITHOUT THE SUPPORT OF THE PEOPLE, THIS GOVERNMENT WILL HAVE NO CHANCE.
Historical Find
DESPITE THEIR MANY DIFFERENCES, JAMES MADISON AND ALEXANDER HAMILTON ARE SOMETIMES REFERRED TO AS THE ODD COUPLE OF THE CONSTITUTION. HAMILTON'S QUICK THINKING AND PASSIONATE SPEECHES WERE AN EXCELLENT MATCH FOR MADISON'S CAREFUL PLANNING.

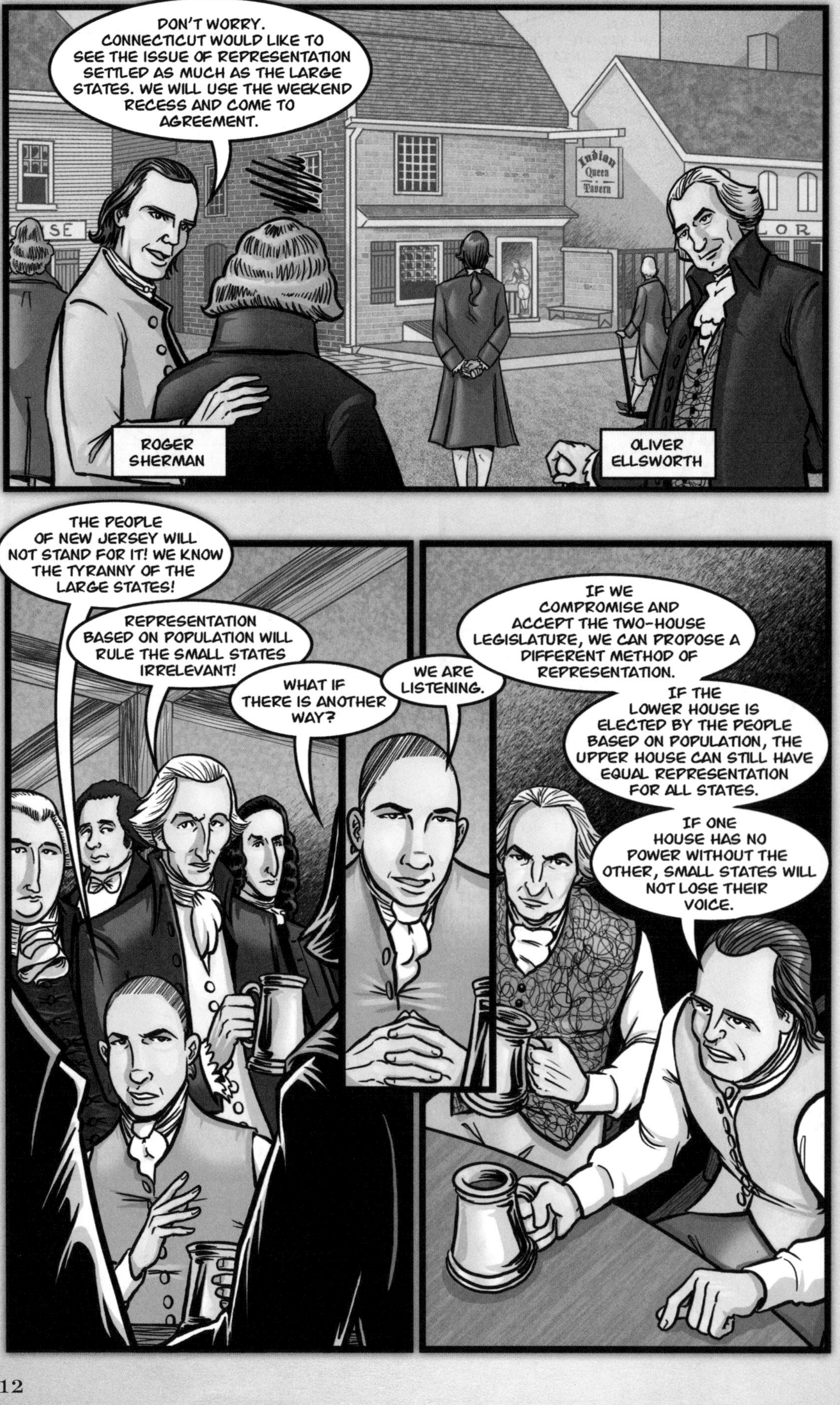

DON'T WORRY. CONNECTICUT WOULD LIKE TO SEE THE ISSUE OF REPRESENTATION SETTLED AS MUCH AS THE LARGE STATES. WE WILL USE THE WEEKEND RECESS AND COME TO AGREEMENT.
Indian Queen Tavern
ROGER SHERMAN
OLIVER ELLSWORTH
THE PEOPLE OF NEW JERSEY WILL NOT STAND FOR IT! WE KNOW THE TYRANNY OF THE LARGE STATES!
REPRESENTATION BASED ON POPULATION WILL RULE THE SMALL STATES IRRELEVANT!
WHAT IF THERE IS ANOTHER WAY?
WE ARE LISTENING.
IF WE COMPROMISE AND ACCEPT THE TWO-HOUSE LEGISLATURE, WE CAN PROPOSE A DIFFERENT METHOD OF REPRESENTATION.
IF THE LOWER HOUSE IS ELECTED BY THE PEOPLE BASED ON POPULATION, THE UPPER HOUSE CAN STILL HAVE EQUAL REPRESENTATION FOR ALL STATES.
IF ONE HOUSE HAS NO POWER WITHOUT THE OTHER, SMALL STATES WILL NOT LOSE THEIR VOICE.

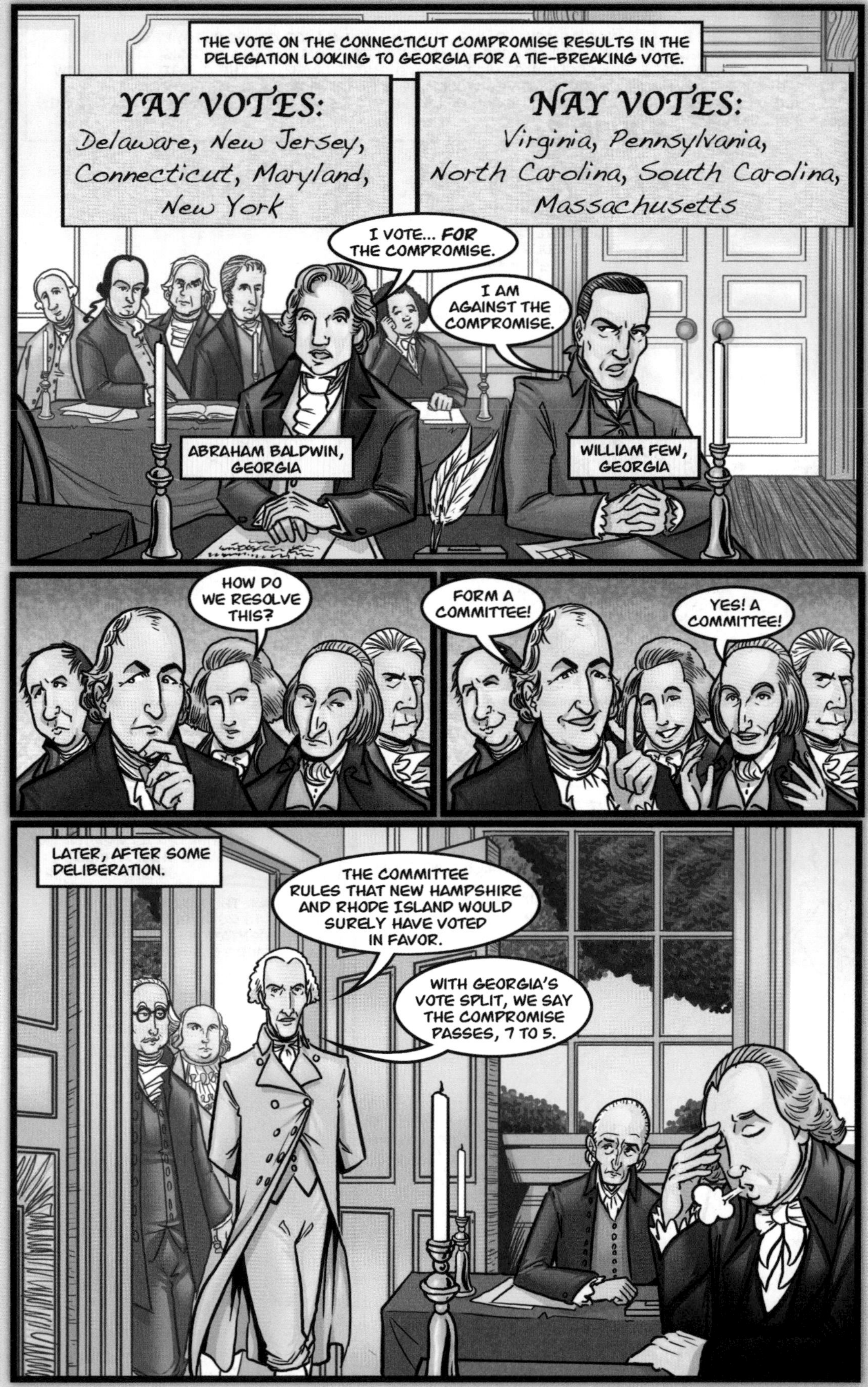
THE VOTE ON THE CONNECTICUT COMPROMISE RESULTS IN THE DELEGATION LOOKING TO GEORGIA FOR A TIE-BREAKING VOTE.
YAY VOTES: Delaware, New Jersey, Connecticut, Maryland, New York
NAY VOTES: Virginia, Pennsylvania, North Carolina, South Carolina, Massachusetts
I VOTE... FOR THE COMPROMISE.
I AM AGAINST THE COMPROMISE.
ABRAHAM BALDWIN, GEORGIA
WILLIAM FEW, GEORGIA
HOW DO WE RESOLVE THIS?
FORM A COMMITTEE!
YES! A COMMITTEE!
LATER, AFTER SOME DELIBERATION.
THE COMMITTEE RULES THAT NEW HAMPSHIRE AND RHODE ISLAND WOULD SURELY HAVE VOTED IN FAVOR.
WITH GEORGIA'S VOTE SPLIT, WE SAY THE COMPROMISE PASSES, 7 TO 5.

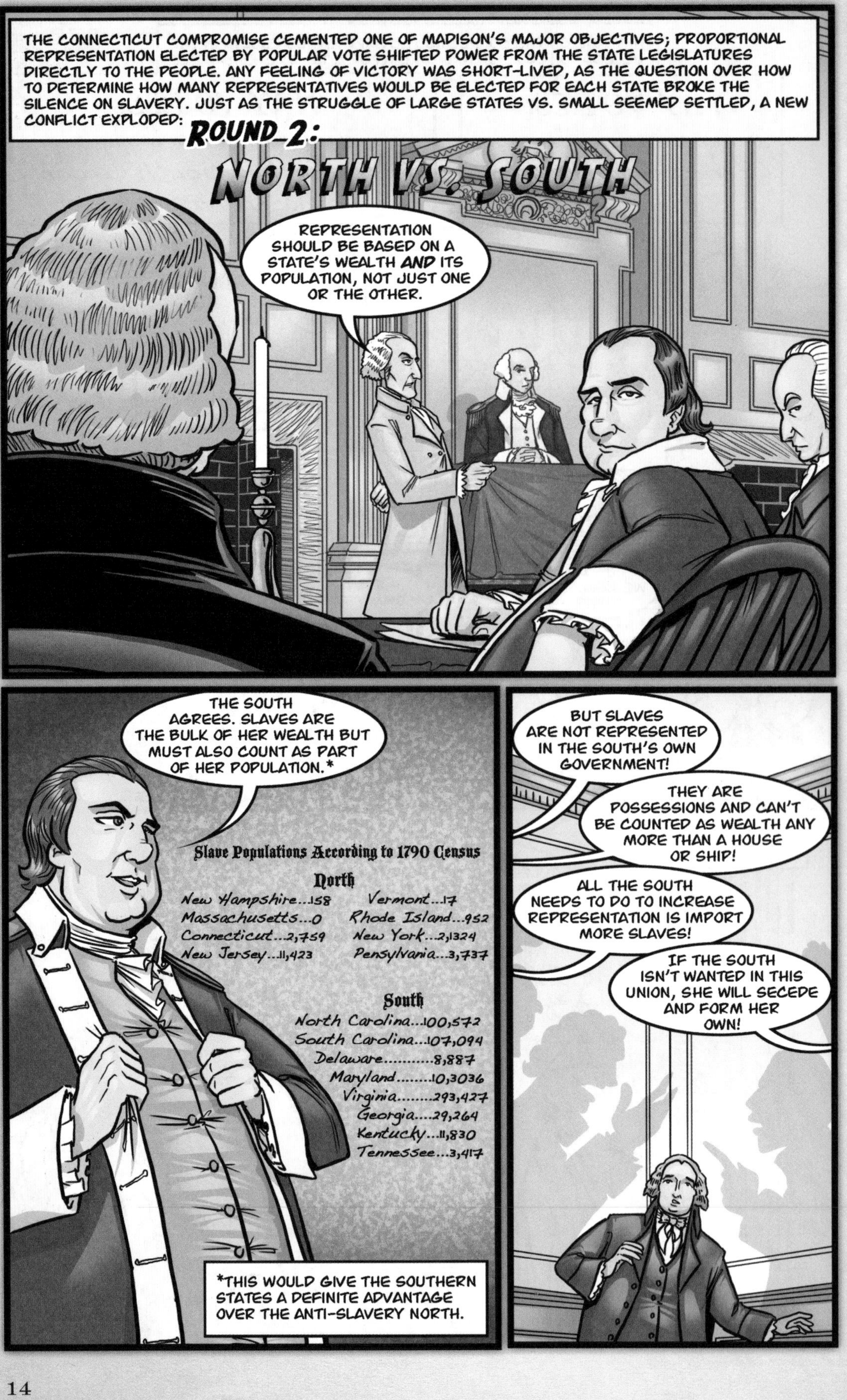
THE CONNECTICUT COMPROMISE CEMENTED ONE OF MADISON'S MAJOR OBJECTIVES; PROPORTIONAL REPRESENTATION ELECTED BY POPULAR VOTE SHIFTED POWER FROM THE STATE LEGISLATURES DIRECTLY TO THE PEOPLE. ANY FEELING OF VICTORY WAS SHORT-LIVED, AS THE QUESTION OVER HOW TO DETERMINE HOW MANY REPRESENTATIVES WOULD BE ELECTED FOR EACH STATE BROKE THE SILENCE ON SLAVERY. JUST AS THE STRUGGLE OF LARGE STATES VS. SMALL SEEMED SETTLED, A NEW CONFLICT EXPLODED:
ROUND 2:
NORTH VS. SOUTH
REPRESENTATION SHOULD BE BASED ON A STATE'S WEALTH **AND** ITS POPULATION, NOT JUST ONE OR THE OTHER.
THE SOUTH AGREES. SLAVES ARE THE BULK OF HER WEALTH BUT MUST ALSO COUNT AS PART OF HER POPULATION.*
Slave Populations According to 1790 Census
North
New Hampshire...158
Massachusetts...0
Connecticut...2,759
New Jersey...11,423
Vermont...17
Rhode Island...952
New York...2,1324
Pensylvania...3,737
South
North Carolina...100,572
South Carolina...107,094
Delaware...........8,887
Maryland........10,3036
Virginia........293,427
Georgia....29,264
Kentucky...11,830
Tennessee...3,417
*THIS WOULD GIVE THE SOUTHERN STATES A DEFINITE ADVANTAGE OVER THE ANTI-SLAVERY NORTH.
BUT SLAVES ARE NOT REPRESENTED IN THE SOUTH'S OWN GOVERNMENT!
THEY ARE POSSESSIONS AND CAN'T BE COUNTED AS WEALTH ANY MORE THAN A HOUSE OR SHIP!
ALL THE SOUTH NEEDS TO DO TO INCREASE REPRESENTATION IS IMPORT MORE SLAVES!
IF THE SOUTH ISN'T WANTED IN THIS UNION, SHE WILL SECEDE AND FORM HER OWN!

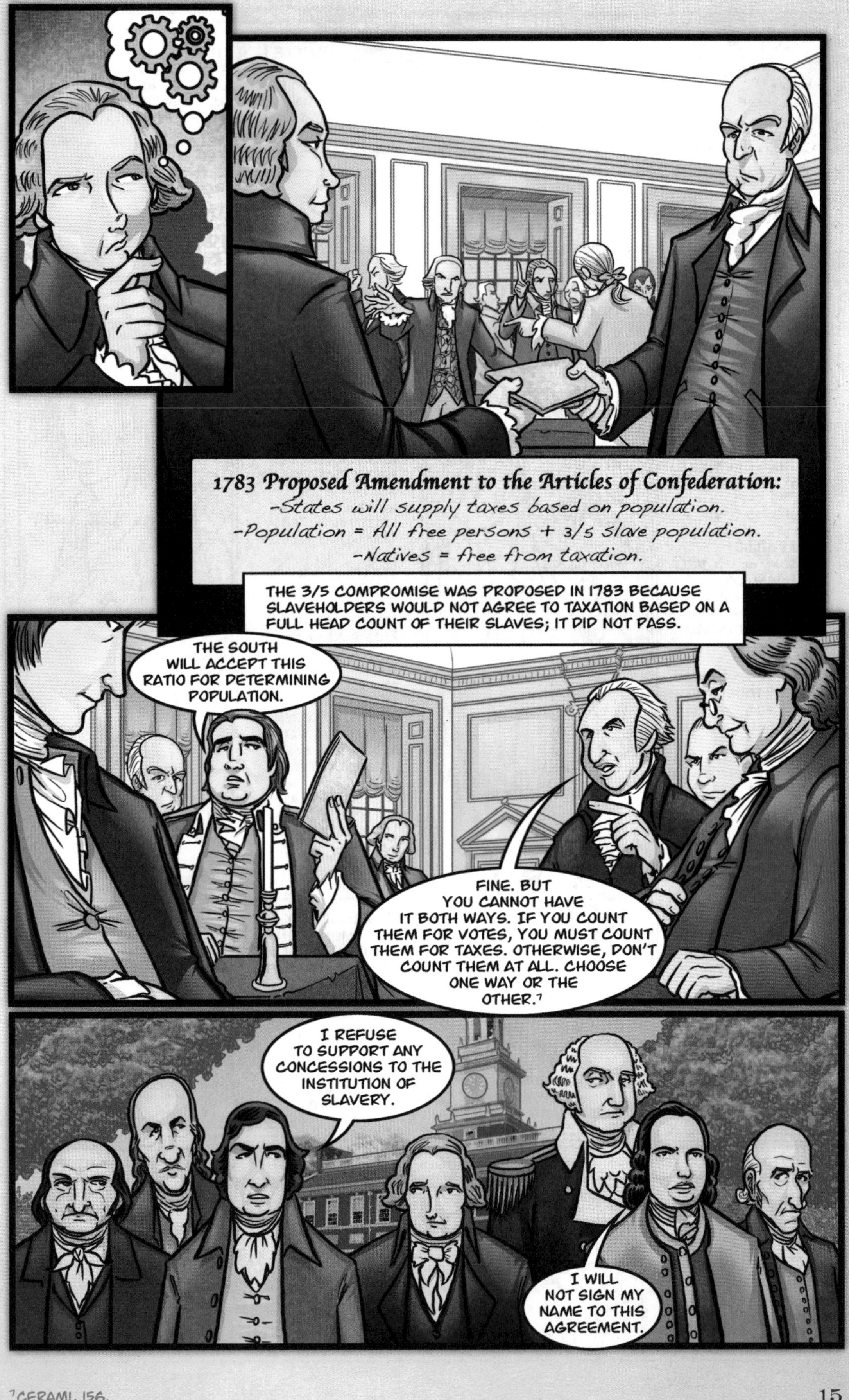
1783 Proposed Amendment to the Articles of Confederation:
-States will supply taxes based on population.
-Population = All free persons + 3/5 slave population.
-Natives = free from taxation.
THE 3/5 COMPROMISE WAS PROPOSED IN 1783 BECAUSE SLAVEHOLDERS WOULD NOT AGREE TO TAXATION BASED ON A FULL HEAD COUNT OF THEIR SLAVES; IT DID NOT PASS.
THE SOUTH WILL ACCEPT THIS RATIO FOR DETERMINING POPULATION.
FINE. BUT YOU CANNOT HAVE IT BOTH WAYS. IF YOU COUNT THEM FOR VOTES, YOU MUST COUNT THEM FOR TAXES. OTHERWISE, DON'T COUNT THEM AT ALL. CHOOSE ONE WAY OR THE OTHER.[7]
I REFUSE TO SUPPORT ANY CONCESSIONS TO THE INSTITUTION OF SLAVERY.
I WILL NOT SIGN MY NAME TO THIS AGREEMENT.

[7] CERAMI, 156.

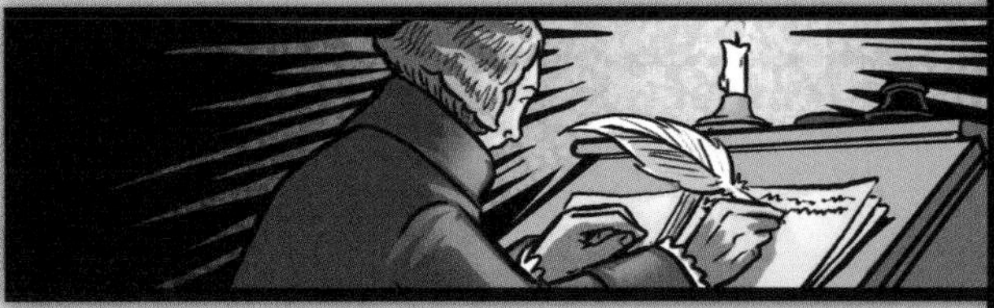

Article I, Section 1: All legislative Powers herein granted shall be vested in a Congress of the United States, which shall consist of a Senate and House of Representatives.

Section 2: The House of Representatives

Term: 2 years

Elected by: popular vote of the people

Age: 25 years or older

Citizenship: must be a U.S. Citizen for at least 7 years and an inhabitant of the state for which they are chosen

Representatives per State: 1 for every 30,000 persons, determined by adding the number of free persons, excluding Indians not taxed, persons*

First census to be taken within 3 years of the first meeting of Congress and repeated every 10 years. Until that time, the states will select the following:

NH 3, MA 8, RI 1, CT 5, NY 6, NJ 4, PA 8, DE 1, MD 6, VA 10, NC 5, SC 5, GA 3

In case of vacancies: The executive authority of the state shall issue Writs of Election to fill vacancies.

Led by: Representatives may elect their own leaders.

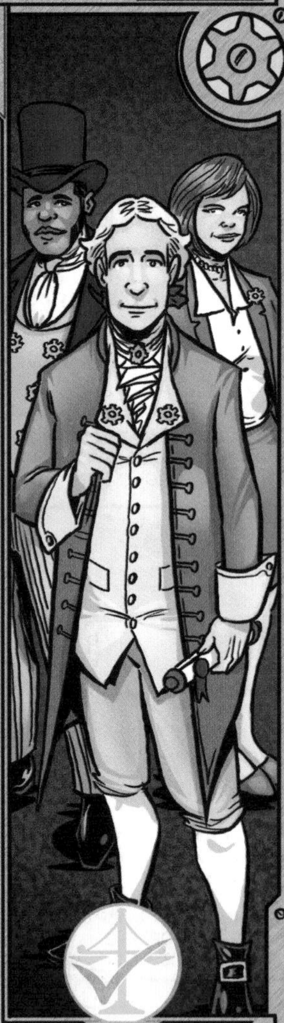

Special Powers: the sole power of Impeachment

Section 3: The Senate

Term: 6 years

Elected by: state legislature**

Age: 30 years or older

Citizenship: must be a U.S. Citizen for at least 9 years and an inhabitant of the state for which they are chosen

Senators per State: 2

Led by: The Vice President of the United States, who has no vote except as a tiebreaker. The Senate may choose all other Officers, as well as a leader in absence of the VP.

Special Powers: the sole power to try all Impeachments

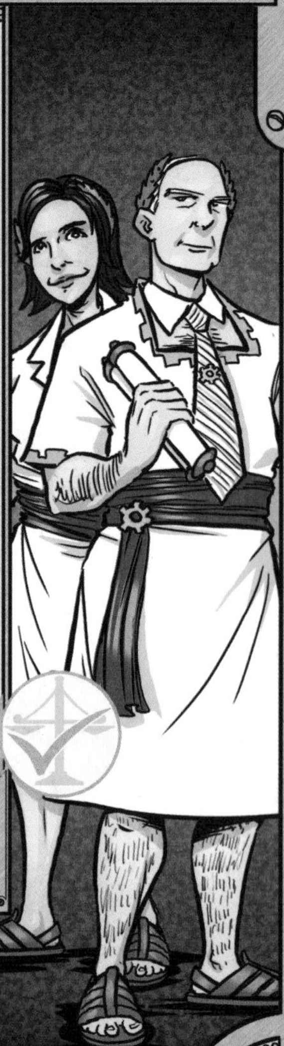

**CHANGED BY 17TH AMENDMENT TO BE ELECTED BY THE POPULAR VOTE OF THE PEOPLE.

*THIS METHOD HAS BEEN AFFECTED OR CHANGED BY THE 14TH, 19TH, AND 24TH AMENDMENTS.

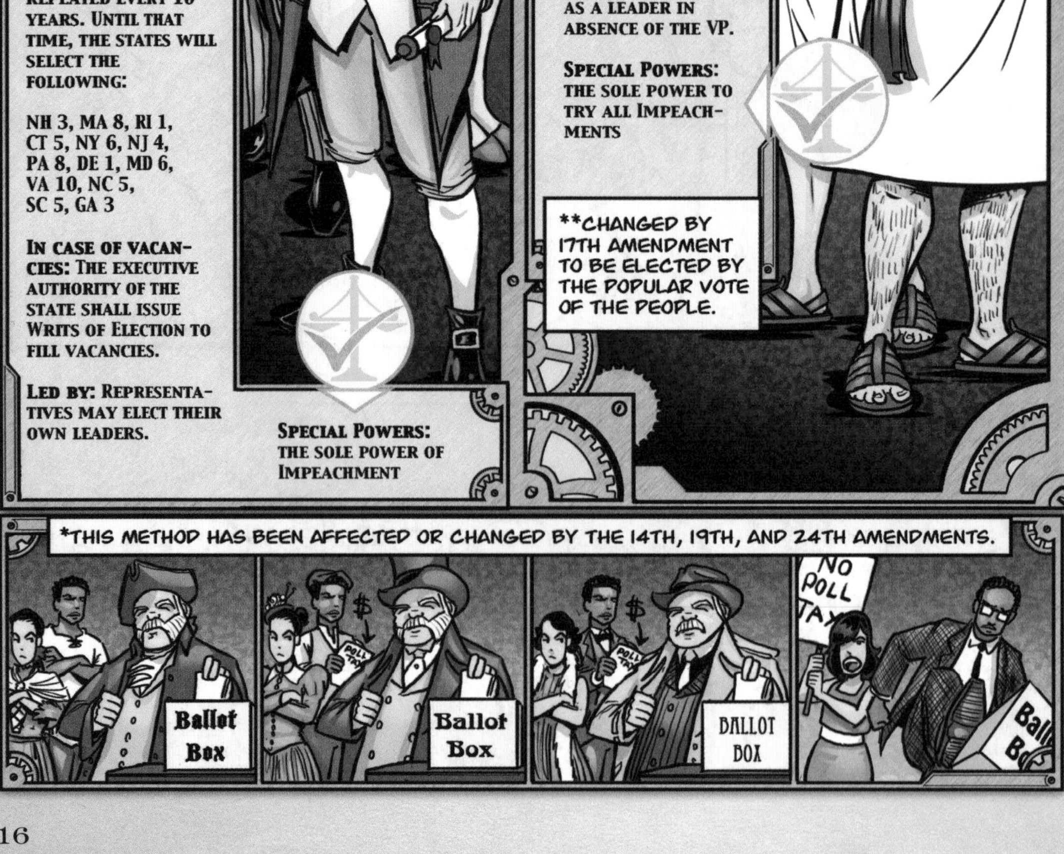
Ballot Box
Ballot Box
BALLOT BOX
NO POLL TAX

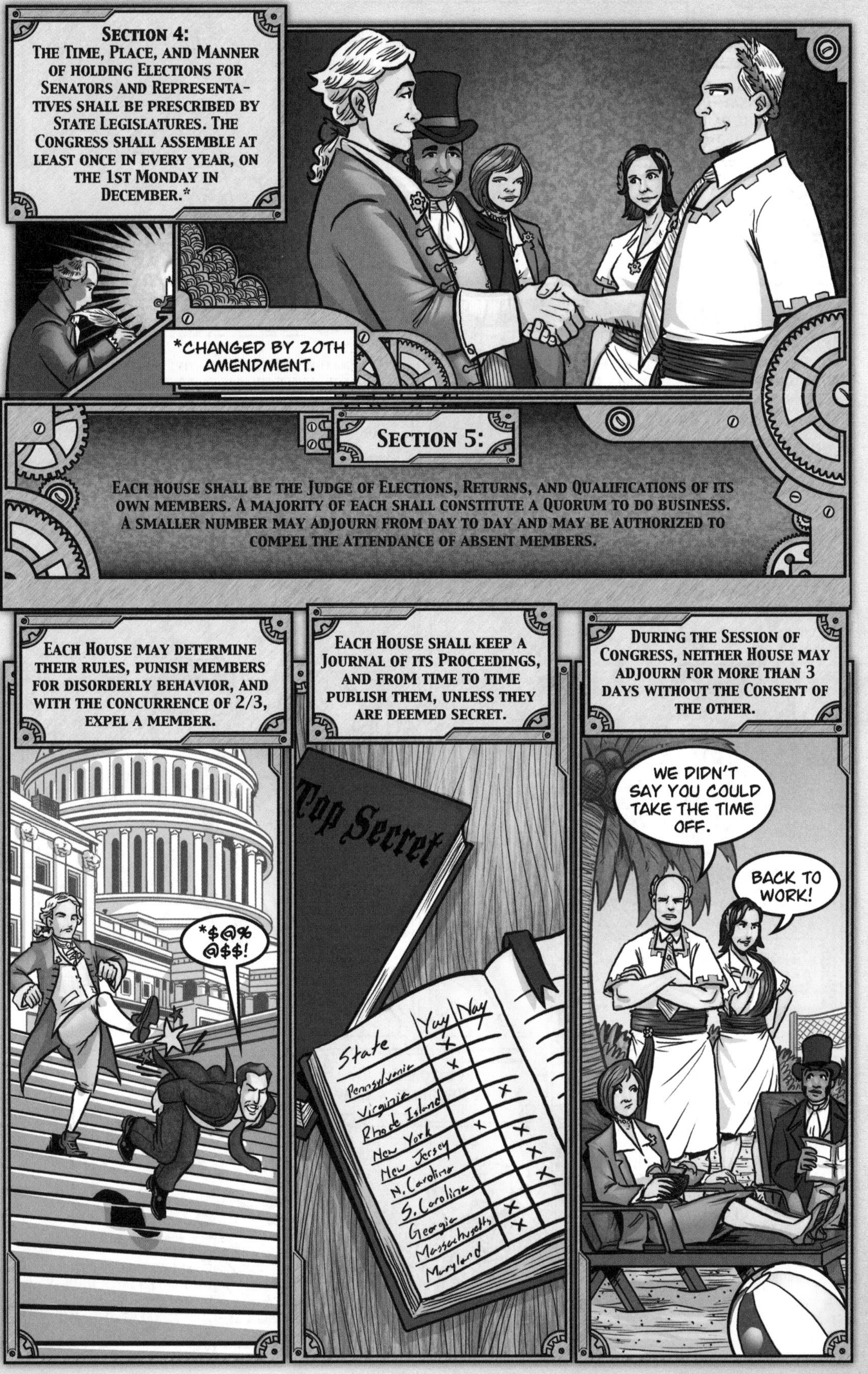

SECTION 4:
THE TIME, PLACE, AND MANNER OF HOLDING ELECTIONS FOR SENATORS AND REPRESENTATIVES SHALL BE PRESCRIBED BY STATE LEGISLATURES. THE CONGRESS SHALL ASSEMBLE AT LEAST ONCE IN EVERY YEAR, ON THE 1ST MONDAY IN DECEMBER.*
*CHANGED BY 20TH AMENDMENT.
SECTION 5:
EACH HOUSE SHALL BE THE JUDGE OF ELECTIONS, RETURNS, AND QUALIFICATIONS OF ITS OWN MEMBERS. A MAJORITY OF EACH SHALL CONSTITUTE A QUORUM TO DO BUSINESS. A SMALLER NUMBER MAY ADJOURN FROM DAY TO DAY AND MAY BE AUTHORIZED TO COMPEL THE ATTENDANCE OF ABSENT MEMBERS.
EACH HOUSE MAY DETERMINE THEIR RULES, PUNISH MEMBERS FOR DISORDERLY BEHAVIOR, AND WITH THE CONCURRENCE OF 2/3, EXPEL A MEMBER.
*$@% @$$!
EACH HOUSE SHALL KEEP A JOURNAL OF ITS PROCEEDINGS, AND FROM TIME TO TIME PUBLISH THEM, UNLESS THEY ARE DEEMED SECRET.
Top Secret
State
Yay
Nay
Pennsylvania
Virginia
Rhode Island
New York
New Jersey
New Carolina
N. Carolina
S. Carolina
Georgia
Massachusetts
Maryland
DURING THE SESSION OF CONGRESS, NEITHER HOUSE MAY ADJOURN FOR MORE THAN 3 DAYS WITHOUT THE CONSENT OF THE OTHER.
WE DIDN'T SAY YOU COULD TAKE THE TIME OFF.
BACK TO WORK!

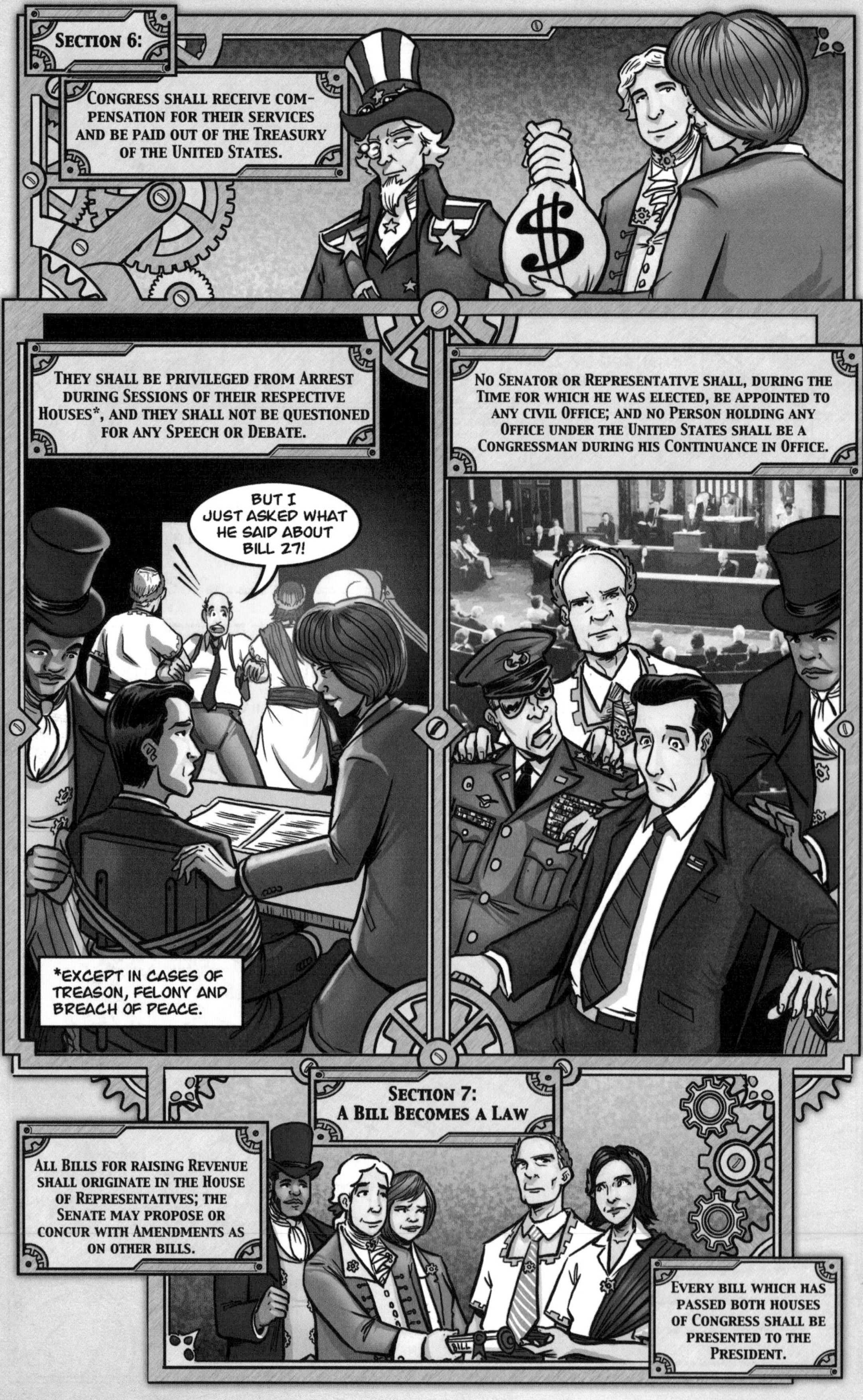

Section 6:
Congress shall receive compensation for their services and be paid out of the Treasury of the United States.
They shall be privileged from Arrest during Sessions of their respective Houses*, and they shall not be questioned for any Speech or Debate.
BUT I JUST ASKED WHAT HE SAID ABOUT BILL 27!
*EXCEPT IN CASES OF TREASON, FELONY AND BREACH OF PEACE.
No Senator or Representative shall, during the Time for which he was elected, be appointed to any civil Office; and no Person holding any Office under the United States shall be a Congressman during his Continuance in Office.
Section 7: A Bill Becomes a Law
All Bills for raising Revenue shall originate in the House of Representatives; the Senate may propose or concur with Amendments as on other bills.
BILL
Every bill which has passed both Houses of Congress shall be presented to the President.

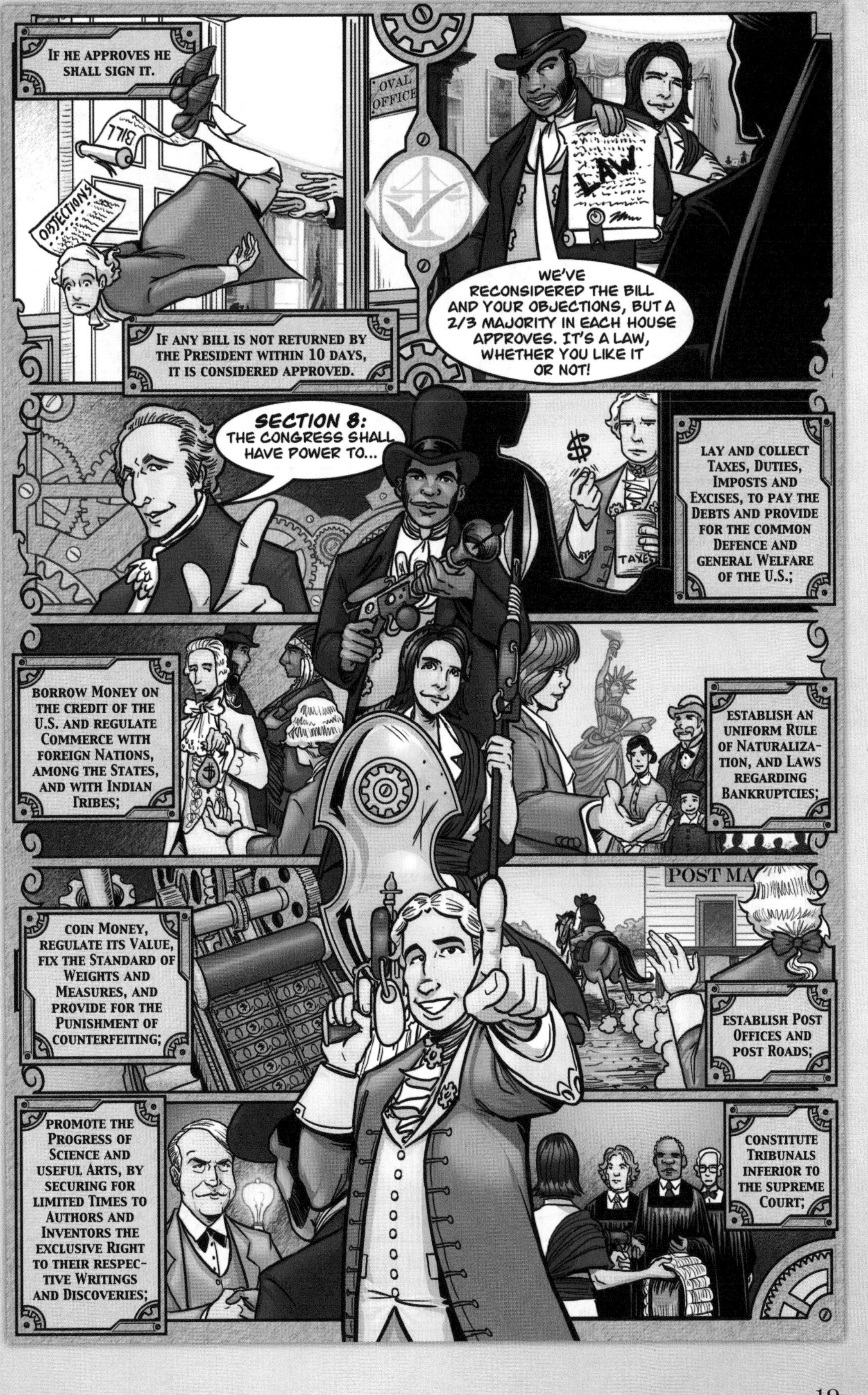

If he approves he shall sign it.
BILL
OBJECTIONS
OVAL OFFICE
LAW
If any bill is not returned by the President within 10 days, it is considered approved.
We've reconsidered the bill and your objections, but a 2/3 majority in each house approves. It's a law, whether you like it or not!
SECTION 8: The Congress shall have power to...
lay and collect Taxes, Duties, Imposts and Excises, to pay the Debts and provide for the common Defence and general Welfare of the U.S.;
TAXES
borrow Money on the credit of the U.S. and regulate Commerce with foreign Nations, among the States, and with Indian Tribes;
establish an uniform Rule of Naturalization, and Laws regarding Bankruptcies;
coin Money, regulate its Value, fix the Standard of Weights and Measures, and provide for the Punishment of counterfeiting;
POST MA
establish Post Offices and post Roads;
promote the Progress of Science and useful Arts, by securing for limited Times to Authors and Inventors the exclusive Right to their respective Writings and Discoveries;
constitute Tribunals inferior to the supreme Court;

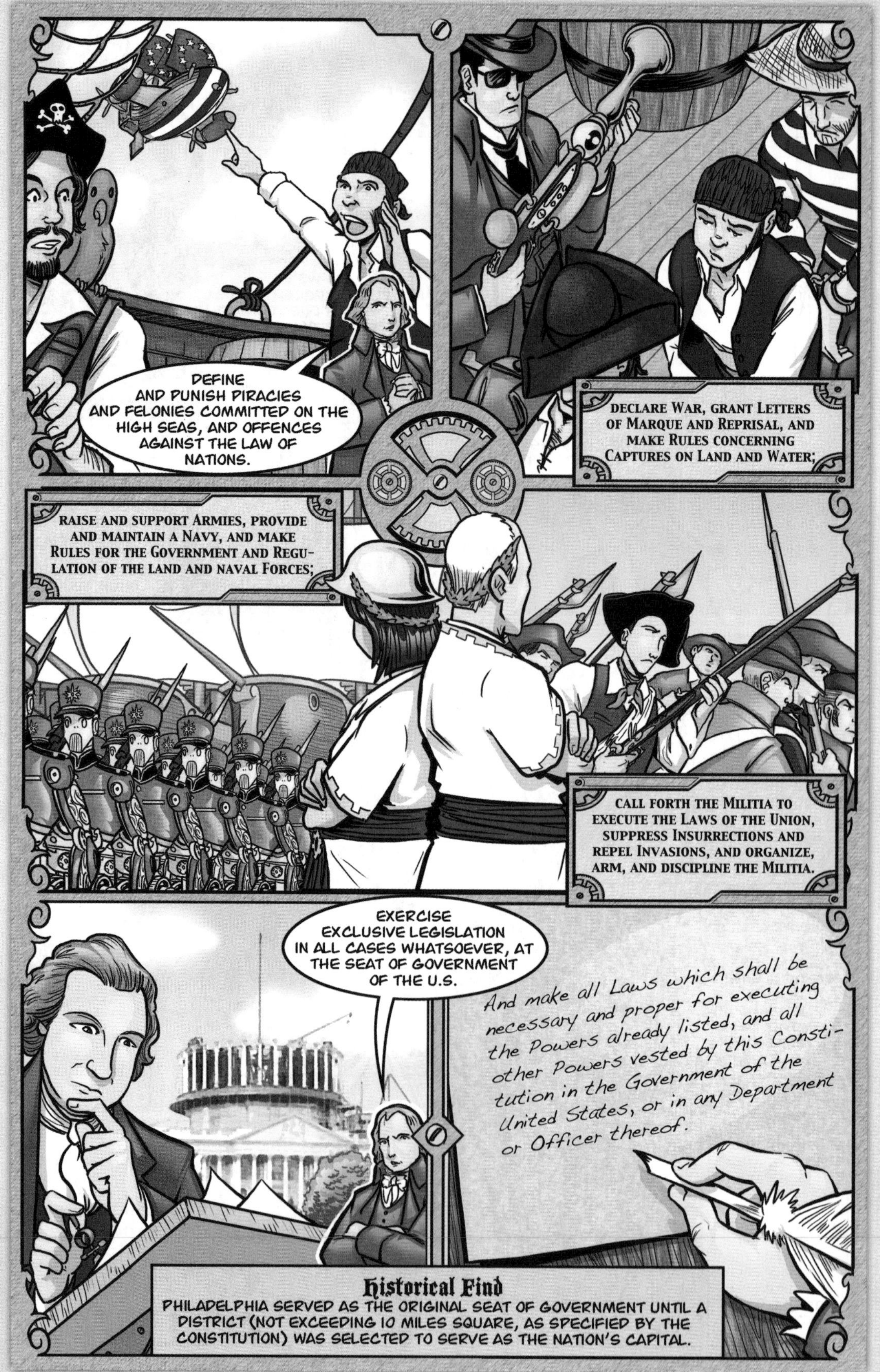
DEFINE AND PUNISH PIRACIES AND FELONIES COMMITTED ON THE HIGH SEAS, AND OFFENCES AGAINST THE LAW OF NATIONS.
DECLARE WAR, GRANT LETTERS OF MARQUE AND REPRISAL, AND MAKE RULES CONCERNING CAPTURES ON LAND AND WATER;
RAISE AND SUPPORT ARMIES, PROVIDE AND MAINTAIN A NAVY, AND MAKE RULES FOR THE GOVERNMENT AND REGULATION OF THE LAND AND NAVAL FORCES;
CALL FORTH THE MILITIA TO EXECUTE THE LAWS OF THE UNION, SUPPRESS INSURRECTIONS AND REPEL INVASIONS, AND ORGANIZE, ARM, AND DISCIPLINE THE MILITIA.
EXERCISE EXCLUSIVE LEGISLATION IN ALL CASES WHATSOEVER, AT THE SEAT OF GOVERNMENT OF THE U.S.
And make all Laws which shall be necessary and proper for executing the Powers already listed, and all other Powers vested by this Constitution in the Government of the United States, or in any Department or Officer thereof.
Historical Find
PHILADELPHIA SERVED AS THE ORIGINAL SEAT OF GOVERNMENT UNTIL A DISTRICT (NOT EXCEEDING 10 MILES SQUARE, AS SPECIFIED BY THE CONSTITUTION) WAS SELECTED TO SERVE AS THE NATION'S CAPITAL.

SECTION 9:
THE MIGRATION OR IMPORTATION OF SUCH PERSONS AS ANY OF THE STATES NOW EXISTING SHALL THINK PROPER TO ADMIT, SHALL NOT BE PROHIBITED BY THE CONGRESS PRIOR TO THE YEAR 1808, BUT A TAX OR DUTY MAY BE IMPOSED ON SUCH IMPORTATION, NOT EXCEEDING $10 FOR EACH PERSON.

Congress may not: Congress may not: Congress may not: Congress may not: Congress may not

Congress may not:

SUSPEND THE PRIVILEGE OF THE WRIT OF HABEAS CORPUS, UNLESS WHEN IN CASES OF REBELLION OR INVASION THE PUBLIC SAFETY MAY REQUIRE IT, NOR PASS A BILL OF ATTAINDER OR EX POST FACTO LAW.

YOU HAVE TO PROVE THAT I DID SOMETHING WRONG OR LET ME GO!

Congress may not:

CREATE A CAPITATION OR OTHER DIRECT TAX, UNLESS IN PROPORTION TO THE CENSUS OR ENUMERATION HEREIN BEFORE DIRECTED TO BE TAKEN.*

*CHANGED BY 16TH AMENDMENT TO ALLOW CONGRESS TO IMPOSE A FEDERAL INCOME TAX.

Congress may not:

LAY TAX OR DUTY ON ARTICLES EXPORTED FROM ANY STATE, NOR GIVE PREFERENCE TO THE PORTS OF ONE STATE OVER THOSE OF ANOTHER; NOR SHALL VESSELS BOUND TO, OR FROM, ONE STATE, BE OBLIGED TO ENTER, CLEAR, OR PAY DUTIES IN ANOTHER.

NEW JERSEY GOODS

ALL OTHER EXPORTS

21

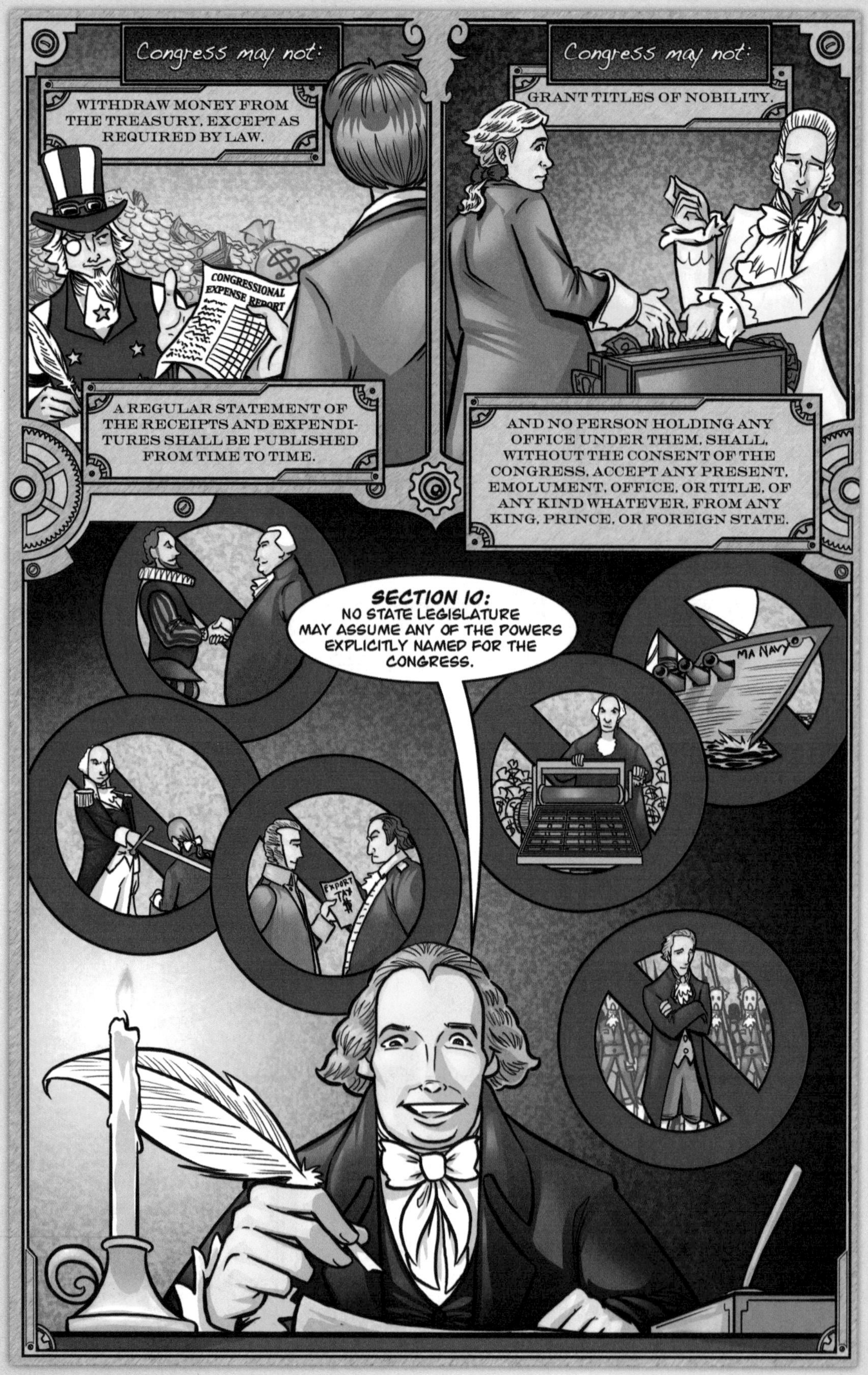
Congress may not:
WITHDRAW MONEY FROM THE TREASURY, EXCEPT AS REQUIRED BY LAW.
CONGRESSIONAL EXPENSE REPORT
A REGULAR STATEMENT OF THE RECEIPTS AND EXPENDITURES SHALL BE PUBLISHED FROM TIME TO TIME.
Congress may not:
GRANT TITLES OF NOBILITY.
AND NO PERSON HOLDING ANY OFFICE UNDER THEM, SHALL, WITHOUT THE CONSENT OF THE CONGRESS, ACCEPT ANY PRESENT, EMOLUMENT, OFFICE, OR TITLE, OF ANY KIND WHATEVER, FROM ANY KING, PRINCE, OR FOREIGN STATE.
SECTION 10:
NO STATE LEGISLATURE MAY ASSUME ANY OF THE POWERS EXPLICITLY NAMED FOR THE CONGRESS.
MA NAVY
EXPORT TAX

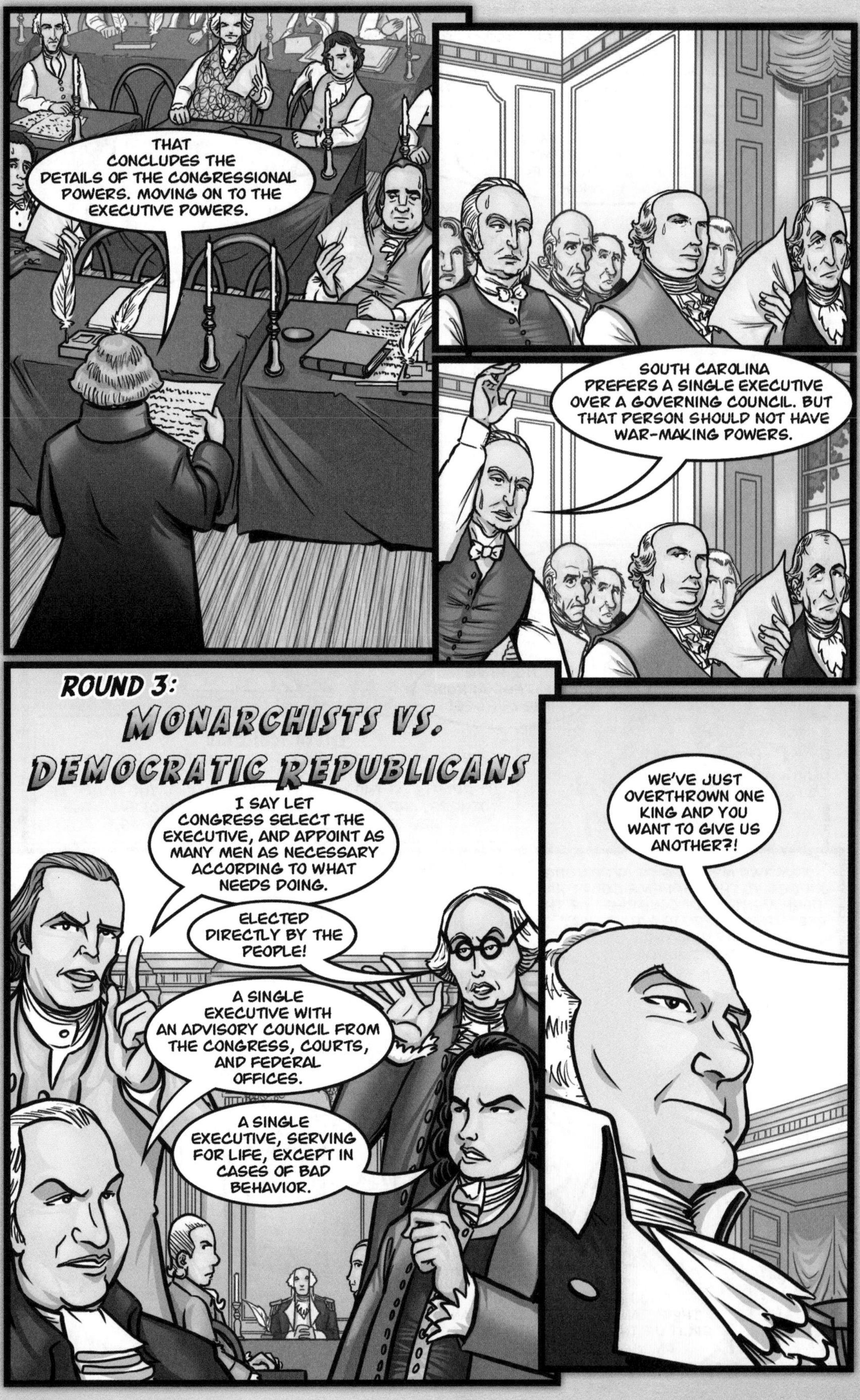
THAT CONCLUDES THE DETAILS OF THE CONGRESSIONAL POWERS. MOVING ON TO THE EXECUTIVE POWERS.
SOUTH CAROLINA PREFERS A SINGLE EXECUTIVE OVER A GOVERNING COUNCIL. BUT THAT PERSON SHOULD NOT HAVE WAR-MAKING POWERS.
ROUND 3:
MONARCHISTS VS. DEMOCRATIC REPUBLICANS
I SAY LET CONGRESS SELECT THE EXECUTIVE, AND APPOINT AS MANY MEN AS NECESSARY ACCORDING TO WHAT NEEDS DOING.
ELECTED DIRECTLY BY THE PEOPLE!
A SINGLE EXECUTIVE WITH AN ADVISORY COUNCIL FROM THE CONGRESS, COURTS, AND FEDERAL OFFICES.
A SINGLE EXECUTIVE, SERVING FOR LIFE, EXCEPT IN CASES OF BAD BEHAVIOR.
WE'VE JUST OVERTHROWN ONE KING AND YOU WANT TO GIVE US ANOTHER?!

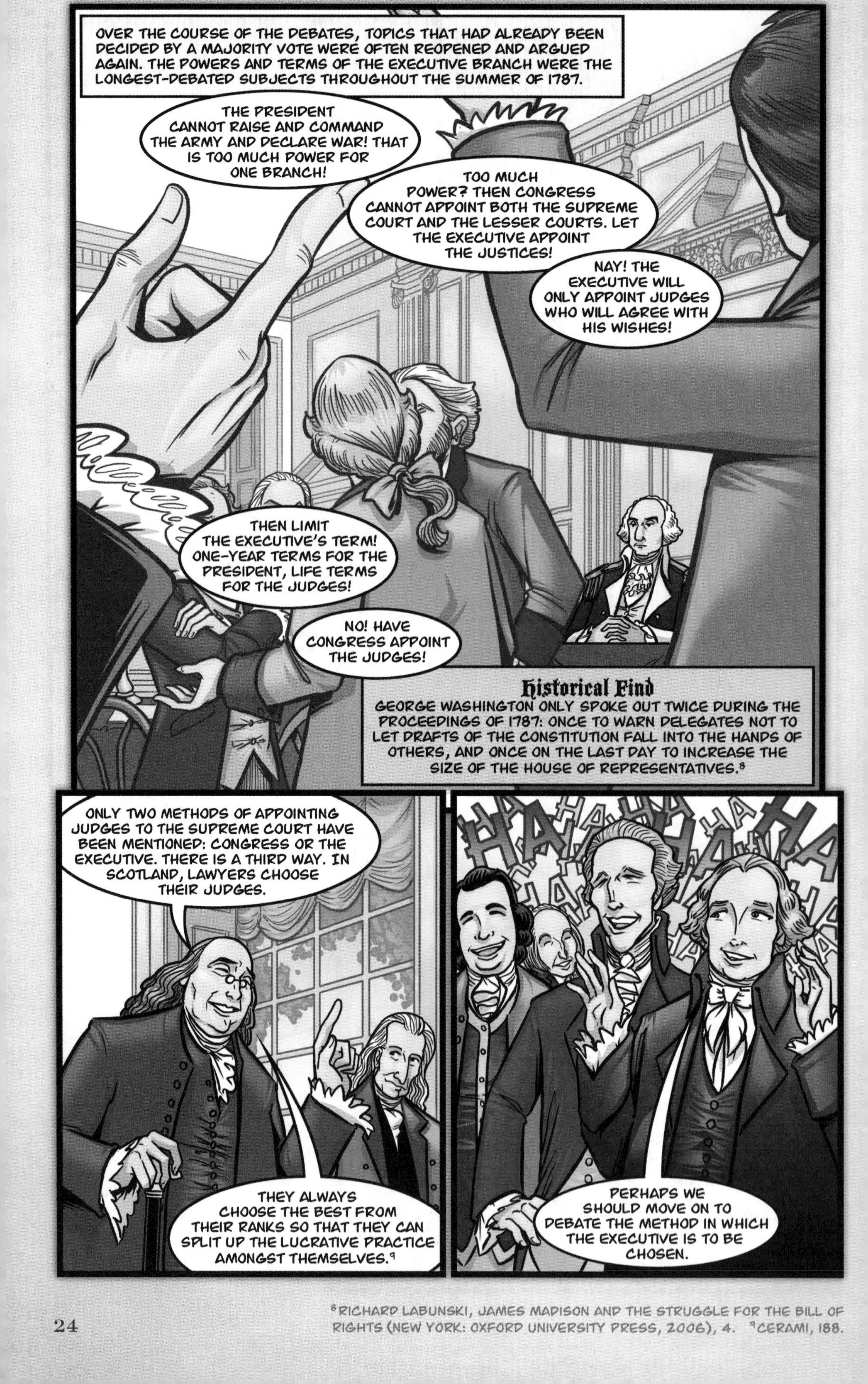
OVER THE COURSE OF THE DEBATES, TOPICS THAT HAD ALREADY BEEN DECIDED BY A MAJORITY VOTE WERE OFTEN REOPENED AND ARGUED AGAIN. THE POWERS AND TERMS OF THE EXECUTIVE BRANCH WERE THE LONGEST-DEBATED SUBJECTS THROUGHOUT THE SUMMER OF 1787.
THE PRESIDENT CANNOT RAISE AND COMMAND THE ARMY AND DECLARE WAR! THAT IS TOO MUCH POWER FOR ONE BRANCH!
TOO MUCH POWER? THEN CONGRESS CANNOT APPOINT BOTH THE SUPREME COURT AND THE LESSER COURTS. LET THE EXECUTIVE APPOINT THE JUSTICES!
NAY! THE EXECUTIVE WILL ONLY APPOINT JUDGES WHO WILL AGREE WITH HIS WISHES!
THEN LIMIT THE EXECUTIVE'S TERM! ONE-YEAR TERMS FOR THE PRESIDENT, LIFE TERMS FOR THE JUDGES!
NO! HAVE CONGRESS APPOINT THE JUDGES!
Historical Find
GEORGE WASHINGTON ONLY SPOKE OUT TWICE DURING THE PROCEEDINGS OF 1787: ONCE TO WARN DELEGATES NOT TO LET DRAFTS OF THE CONSTITUTION FALL INTO THE HANDS OF OTHERS, AND ONCE ON THE LAST DAY TO INCREASE THE SIZE OF THE HOUSE OF REPRESENTATIVES.[8]
ONLY TWO METHODS OF APPOINTING JUDGES TO THE SUPREME COURT HAVE BEEN MENTIONED: CONGRESS OR THE EXECUTIVE. THERE IS A THIRD WAY. IN SCOTLAND, LAWYERS CHOOSE THEIR JUDGES.
THEY ALWAYS CHOOSE THE BEST FROM THEIR RANKS SO THAT THEY CAN SPLIT UP THE LUCRATIVE PRACTICE AMONGST THEMSELVES.[9]
HA HA HA
PERHAPS WE SHOULD MOVE ON TO DEBATE THE METHOD IN WHICH THE EXECUTIVE IS TO BE CHOSEN.

[8] RICHARD LABUNSKI, JAMES MADISON AND THE STRUGGLE FOR THE BILL OF RIGHTS (NEW YORK: OXFORD UNIVERSITY PRESS, 2006), 4. [9] CERAMI, 188.

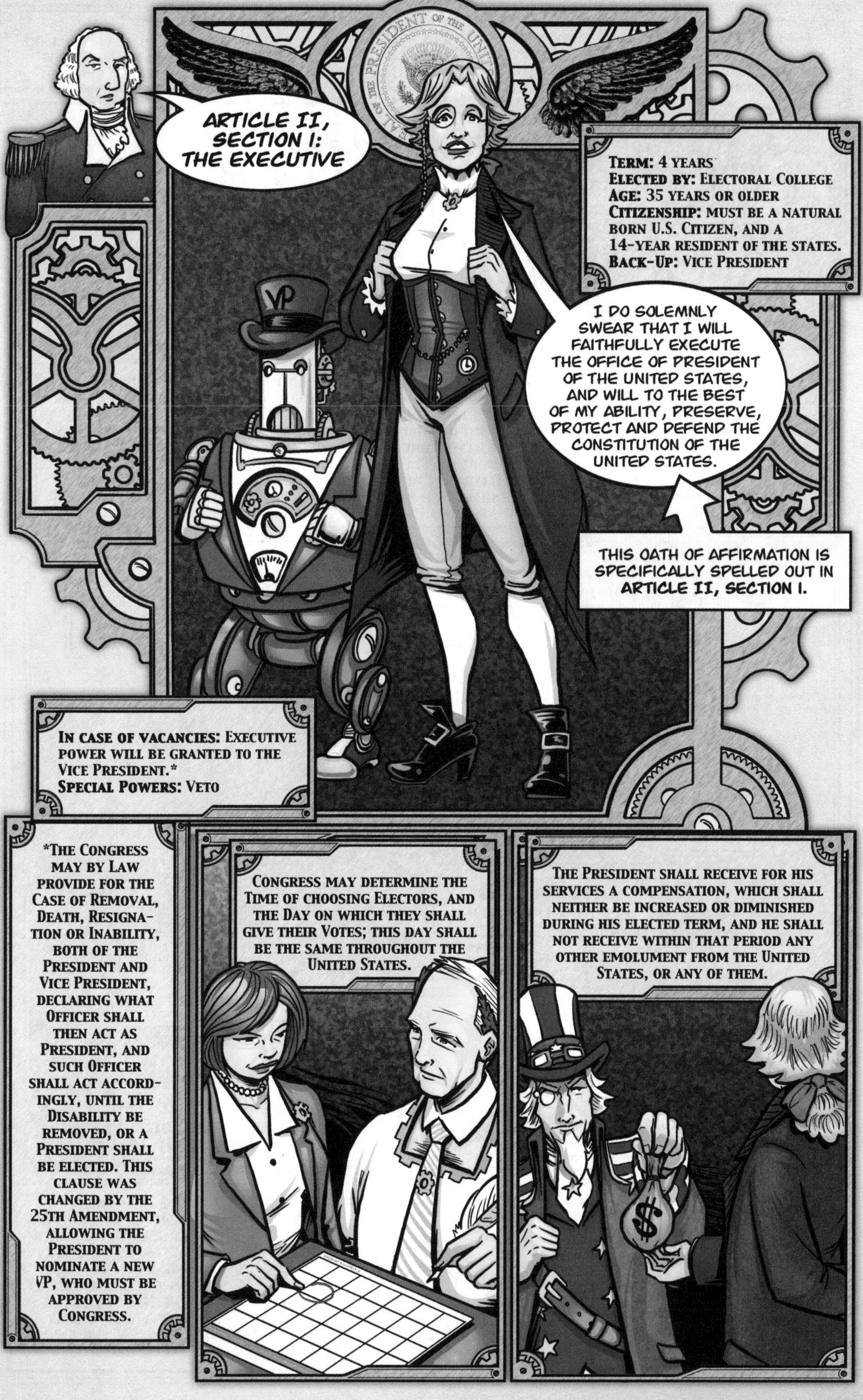
ARTICLE II, SECTION I: THE EXECUTIVE
TERM: 4 YEARS
ELECTED BY: ELECTORAL COLLEGE
AGE: 35 YEARS OR OLDER
CITIZENSHIP: MUST BE A NATURAL BORN U.S. CITIZEN, AND A 14-YEAR RESIDENT OF THE STATES.
BACK-UP: VICE PRESIDENT
VP
I DO SOLEMNLY SWEAR THAT I WILL FAITHFULLY EXECUTE THE OFFICE OF PRESIDENT OF THE UNITED STATES, AND WILL TO THE BEST OF MY ABILITY, PRESERVE, PROTECT AND DEFEND THE CONSTITUTION OF THE UNITED STATES.
THIS OATH OF AFFIRMATION IS SPECIFICALLY SPELLED OUT IN ARTICLE II, SECTION I.
IN CASE OF VACANCIES: EXECUTIVE POWER WILL BE GRANTED TO THE VICE PRESIDENT.*
SPECIAL POWERS: VETO
*THE CONGRESS MAY BY LAW PROVIDE FOR THE CASE OF REMOVAL, DEATH, RESIGNATION OR INABILITY, BOTH OF THE PRESIDENT AND VICE PRESIDENT, DECLARING WHAT OFFICER SHALL THEN ACT AS PRESIDENT, AND SUCH OFFICER SHALL ACT ACCORDINGLY, UNTIL THE DISABILITY BE REMOVED, OR A PRESIDENT SHALL BE ELECTED. THIS CLAUSE WAS CHANGED BY THE 25TH AMENDMENT, ALLOWING THE PRESIDENT TO NOMINATE A NEW VP, WHO MUST BE APPROVED BY CONGRESS.
CONGRESS MAY DETERMINE THE TIME OF CHOOSING ELECTORS, AND THE DAY ON WHICH THEY SHALL GIVE THEIR VOTES; THIS DAY SHALL BE THE SAME THROUGHOUT THE UNITED STATES.
THE PRESIDENT SHALL RECEIVE FOR HIS SERVICES A COMPENSATION, WHICH SHALL NEITHER BE INCREASED OR DIMINISHED DURING HIS ELECTED TERM, AND HE SHALL NOT RECEIVE WITHIN THAT PERIOD ANY OTHER EMOLUMENT FROM THE UNITED STATES, OR ANY OF THEM.
$

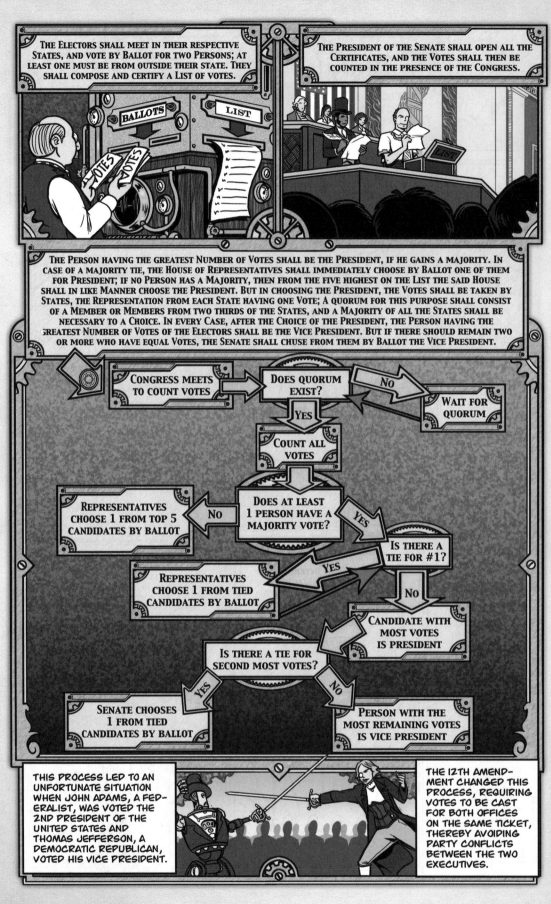

THE ELECTORS SHALL MEET IN THEIR RESPECTIVE STATES, AND VOTE BY BALLOT FOR TWO PERSONS; AT LEAST ONE MUST BE FROM OUTSIDE THEIR STATE. THEY SHALL COMPOSE AND CERTIFY A LIST OF VOTES.

BALLOTS

LIST

THE PRESIDENT OF THE SENATE SHALL OPEN ALL THE CERTIFICATES, AND THE VOTES SHALL THEN BE COUNTED IN THE PRESENCE OF THE CONGRESS.

LIST

THE PERSON HAVING THE GREATEST NUMBER OF VOTES SHALL BE THE PRESIDENT, IF HE GAINS A MAJORITY. IN CASE OF A MAJORITY TIE, THE HOUSE OF REPRESENTATIVES SHALL IMMEDIATELY CHOOSE BY BALLOT ONE OF THEM FOR PRESIDENT; IF NO PERSON HAS A MAJORITY, THEN FROM THE FIVE HIGHEST ON THE LIST THE SAID HOUSE SHALL IN LIKE MANNER CHOOSE THE PRESIDENT. BUT IN CHOOSING THE PRESIDENT, THE VOTES SHALL BE TAKEN BY STATES, THE REPRESENTATION FROM EACH STATE HAVING ONE VOTE; A QUORUM FOR THIS PURPOSE SHALL CONSIST OF A MEMBER OR MEMBERS FROM TWO THIRDS OF THE STATES, AND A MAJORITY OF ALL THE STATES SHALL BE NECESSARY TO A CHOICE. IN EVERY CASE, AFTER THE CHOICE OF THE PRESIDENT, THE PERSON HAVING THE GREATEST NUMBER OF VOTES OF THE ELECTORS SHALL BE THE VICE PRESIDENT. BUT IF THERE SHOULD REMAIN TWO OR MORE WHO HAVE EQUAL VOTES, THE SENATE SHALL CHUSE FROM THEM BY BALLOT THE VICE PRESIDENT.

CONGRESS MEETS TO COUNT VOTES → DOES QUORUM EXIST? → NO → WAIT FOR QUORUM

YES

COUNT ALL VOTES

REPRESENTATIVES CHOOSE 1 FROM TOP 5 CANDIDATES BY BALLOT ← NO ← DOES AT LEAST 1 PERSON HAVE A MAJORITY VOTE? → YES → IS THERE A TIE FOR #1?

YES

REPRESENTATIVES CHOOSE 1 FROM TIED CANDIDATES BY BALLOT

NO

CANDIDATE WITH MOST VOTES IS PRESIDENT

IS THERE A TIE FOR SECOND MOST VOTES?

YES → SENATE CHOOSES 1 FROM TIED CANDIDATES BY BALLOT

NO → PERSON WITH THE MOST REMAINING VOTES IS VICE PRESIDENT

THIS PROCESS LED TO AN UNFORTUNATE SITUATION WHEN JOHN ADAMS, A FEDERALIST, WAS VOTED THE 2ND PRESIDENT OF THE UNITED STATES AND THOMAS JEFFERSON, A DEMOCRATIC REPUBLICAN, VOTED HIS VICE PRESIDENT.

THE 12TH AMENDMENT CHANGED THIS PROCESS, REQUIRING VOTES TO BE CAST FOR BOTH OFFICES ON THE SAME TICKET, THEREBY AVOIDING PARTY CONFLICTS BETWEEN THE TWO EXECUTIVES.

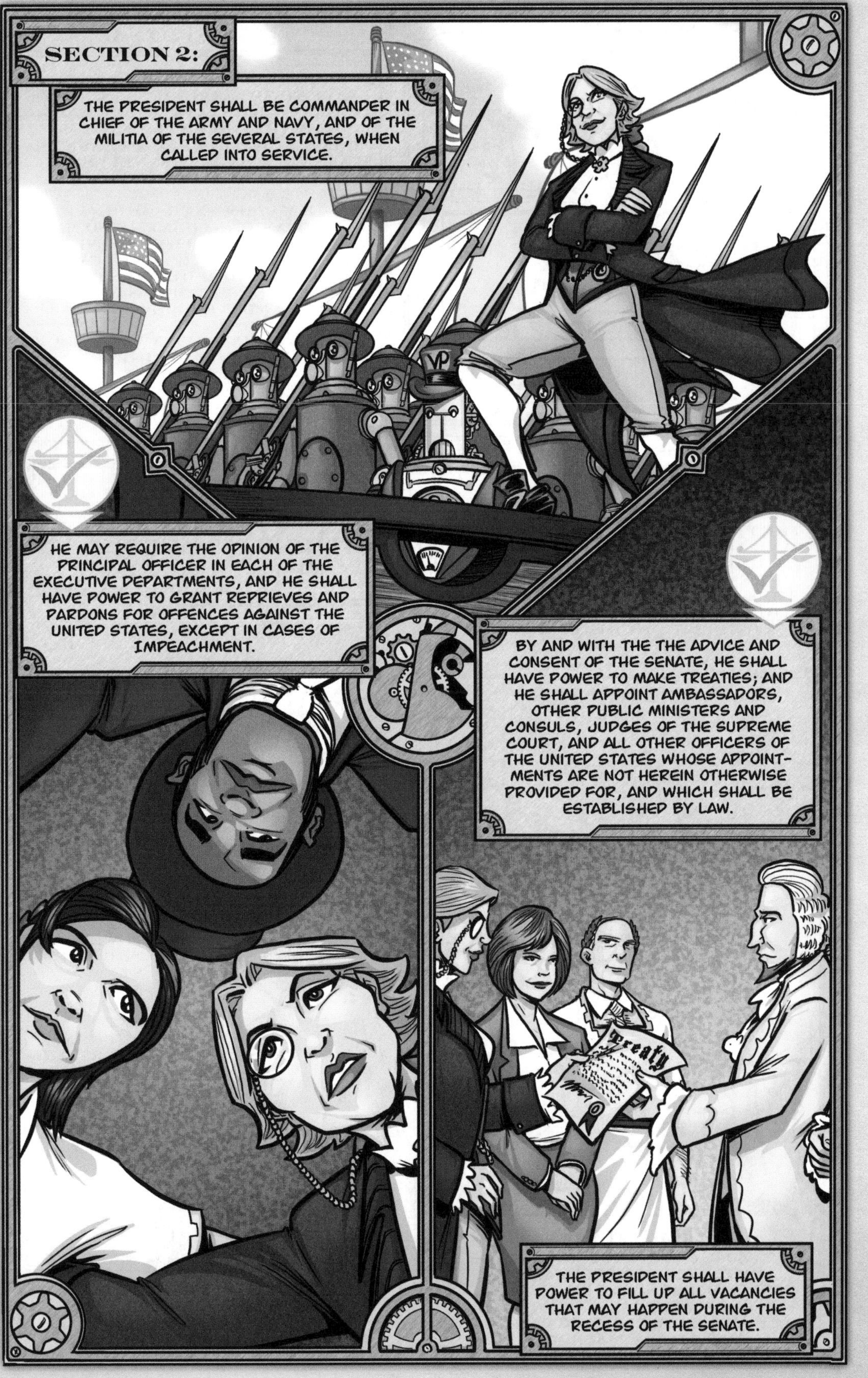
SECTION 2:
THE PRESIDENT SHALL BE COMMANDER IN CHIEF OF THE ARMY AND NAVY, AND OF THE MILITIA OF THE SEVERAL STATES, WHEN CALLED INTO SERVICE.
VP
HE MAY REQUIRE THE OPINION OF THE PRINCIPAL OFFICER IN EACH OF THE EXECUTIVE DEPARTMENTS, AND HE SHALL HAVE POWER TO GRANT REPRIEVES AND PARDONS FOR OFFENCES AGAINST THE UNITED STATES, EXCEPT IN CASES OF IMPEACHMENT.
BY AND WITH THE THE ADVICE AND CONSENT OF THE SENATE, HE SHALL HAVE POWER TO MAKE TREATIES; AND HE SHALL APPOINT AMBASSADORS, OTHER PUBLIC MINISTERS AND CONSULS, JUDGES OF THE SUPREME COURT, AND ALL OTHER OFFICERS OF THE UNITED STATES WHOSE APPOINTMENTS ARE NOT HEREIN OTHERWISE PROVIDED FOR, AND WHICH SHALL BE ESTABLISHED BY LAW.
Treaty
THE PRESIDENT SHALL HAVE POWER TO FILL UP ALL VACANCIES THAT MAY HAPPEN DURING THE RECESS OF THE SENATE.

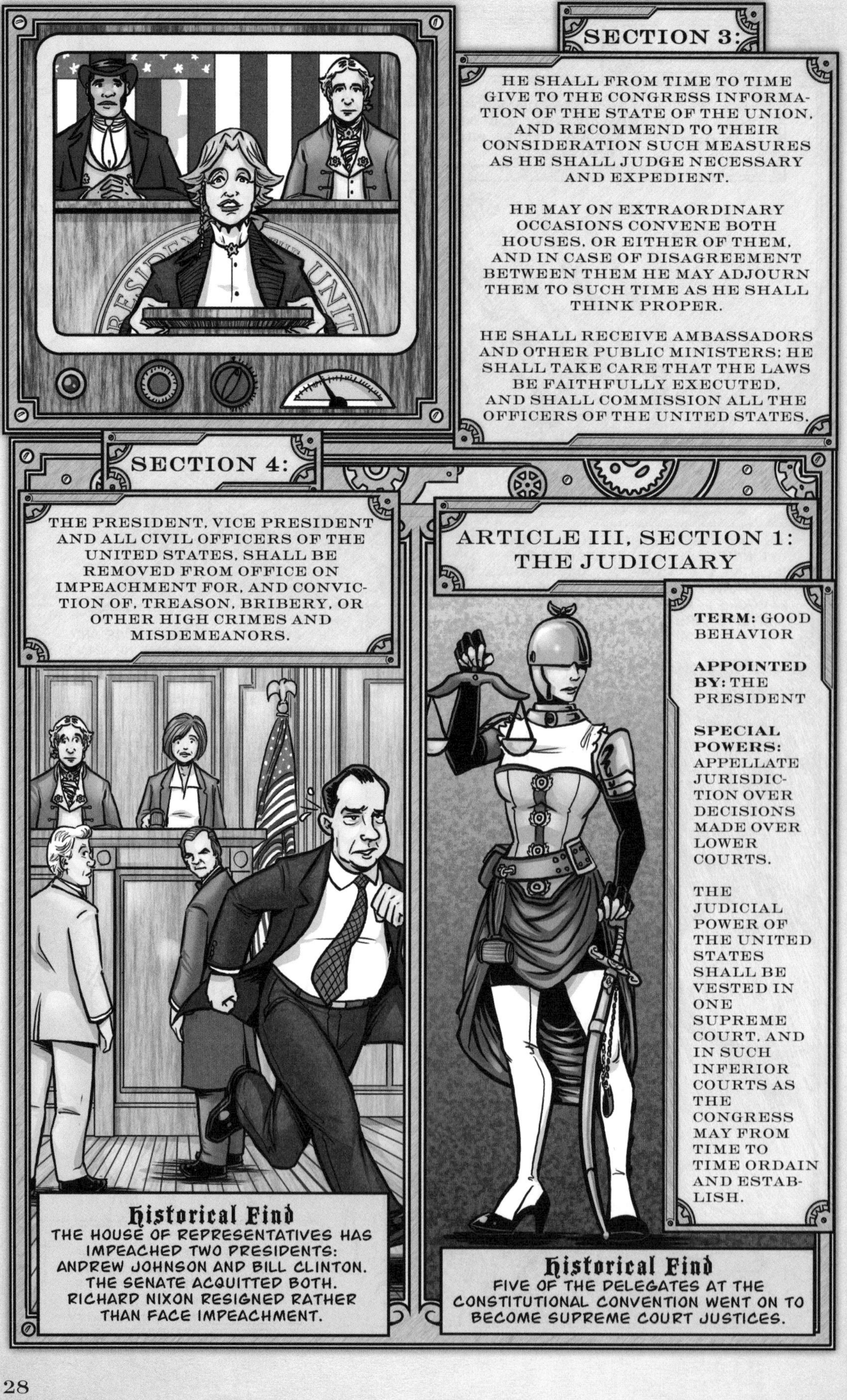
SECTION 3:
HE SHALL FROM TIME TO TIME GIVE TO THE CONGRESS INFORMATION OF THE STATE OF THE UNION, AND RECOMMEND TO THEIR CONSIDERATION SUCH MEASURES AS HE SHALL JUDGE NECESSARY AND EXPEDIENT.
HE MAY ON EXTRAORDINARY OCCASIONS CONVENE BOTH HOUSES, OR EITHER OF THEM, AND IN CASE OF DISAGREEMENT BETWEEN THEM HE MAY ADJOURN THEM TO SUCH TIME AS HE SHALL THINK PROPER.
HE SHALL RECEIVE AMBASSADORS AND OTHER PUBLIC MINISTERS; HE SHALL TAKE CARE THAT THE LAWS BE FAITHFULLY EXECUTED, AND SHALL COMMISSION ALL THE OFFICERS OF THE UNITED STATES.
SECTION 4:
THE PRESIDENT, VICE PRESIDENT AND ALL CIVIL OFFICERS OF THE UNITED STATES, SHALL BE REMOVED FROM OFFICE ON IMPEACHMENT FOR, AND CONVICTION OF, TREASON, BRIBERY, OR OTHER HIGH CRIMES AND MISDEMEANORS.
Historical Find
THE HOUSE OF REPRESENTATIVES HAS IMPEACHED TWO PRESIDENTS: ANDREW JOHNSON AND BILL CLINTON. THE SENATE ACQUITTED BOTH. RICHARD NIXON RESIGNED RATHER THAN FACE IMPEACHMENT.
ARTICLE III, SECTION 1: THE JUDICIARY
TERM: GOOD BEHAVIOR
APPOINTED BY: THE PRESIDENT
SPECIAL POWERS: APPELLATE JURISDICTION OVER DECISIONS MADE OVER LOWER COURTS.
THE JUDICIAL POWER OF THE UNITED STATES SHALL BE VESTED IN ONE SUPREME COURT, AND IN SUCH INFERIOR COURTS AS THE CONGRESS MAY FROM TIME TO TIME ORDAIN AND ESTABLISH.
Historical Find
FIVE OF THE DELEGATES AT THE CONSTITUTIONAL CONVENTION WENT ON TO BECOME SUPREME COURT JUSTICES.

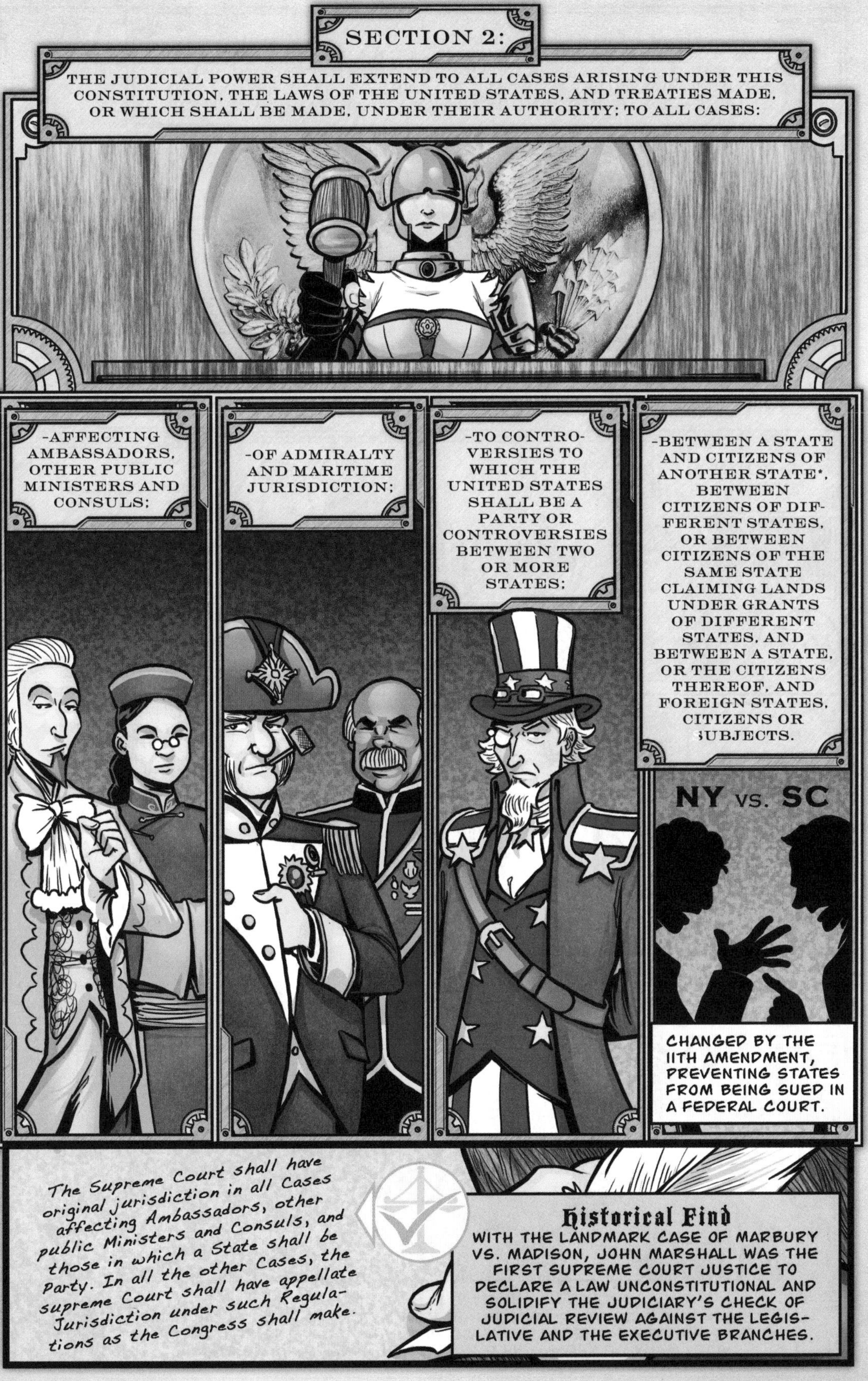
SECTION 2:
THE JUDICIAL POWER SHALL EXTEND TO ALL CASES ARISING UNDER THIS CONSTITUTION, THE LAWS OF THE UNITED STATES, AND TREATIES MADE, OR WHICH SHALL BE MADE, UNDER THEIR AUTHORITY; TO ALL CASES:
-AFFECTING AMBASSADORS, OTHER PUBLIC MINISTERS AND CONSULS;
-OF ADMIRALTY AND MARITIME JURISDICTION;
-TO CONTROVERSIES TO WHICH THE UNITED STATES SHALL BE A PARTY OR CONTROVERSIES BETWEEN TWO OR MORE STATES;
-BETWEEN A STATE AND CITIZENS OF ANOTHER STATE*, BETWEEN CITIZENS OF DIFFERENT STATES, OR BETWEEN CITIZENS OF THE SAME STATE CLAIMING LANDS UNDER GRANTS OF DIFFERENT STATES, AND BETWEEN A STATE, OR THE CITIZENS THEREOF, AND FOREIGN STATES, CITIZENS OR SUBJECTS.
NY VS. SC
CHANGED BY THE 11TH AMENDMENT, PREVENTING STATES FROM BEING SUED IN A FEDERAL COURT.
The Supreme Court shall have original jurisdiction in all Cases affecting Ambassadors, other public Ministers and Consuls, and those in which a State shall be Party. In all the other Cases, the supreme Court shall have appellate Jurisdiction under such Regulations as the Congress shall make.
Historical Find
WITH THE LANDMARK CASE OF MARBURY VS. MADISON, JOHN MARSHALL WAS THE FIRST SUPREME COURT JUSTICE TO DECLARE A LAW UNCONSTITUTIONAL AND SOLIDIFY THE JUDICIARY'S CHECK OF JUDICIAL REVIEW AGAINST THE LEGISLATIVE AND THE EXECUTIVE BRANCHES.

THE TRIAL OF ALL CRIMES, EXCEPT IN CASES OF IMPEACHMENT, SHALL BE BY JURY*; AND SUCH TRIAL SHALL BE HELD IN THE STATE WHERE THE SAID CRIMES SHALL HAVE BEEN COMMITTED; BUT WHEN NOT COMMITTED WITHIN ANY STATE, THE TRIAL SHALL BE AT SUCH PLACE OR PLACES AS THE CONGRESS MAY BY LAW HAVE DIRECTED.

THE RIGHT TO TRIAL BY JURY WAS FURTHER DEFINED AND STRENGTHENED BY THE 6TH, 7TH, 8TH, AND 9TH AMENDMENTS.

SECTION 3: TREASON

WEST POINT DEFENSE PLANS

TREASON AGAINST THE UNITED STATES SHALL CONSIST ONLY IN LEVYING WAR AGAINST THEM, OR IN ADHERING TO THEIR ENEMIES, GIVING THEM AID AND COMFORT.

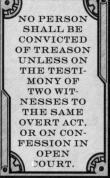

NO PERSON SHALL BE CONVICTED OF TREASON UNLESS ON THE TESTIMONY OF TWO WITNESSES TO THE SAME OVERT ACT, OR ON CONFESSION IN OPEN COURT.

THE CONGRESS SHALL HAVE POWER TO DECLARE THE PUNISHMENT OF TREASON, BUT NO ATTAINDER OF TREASON SHALL WORK CORRUPTION OF BLOOD, OR FORFEITURE EXCEPT DURING THE LIFE OF THE PERSON ATTAINTED.

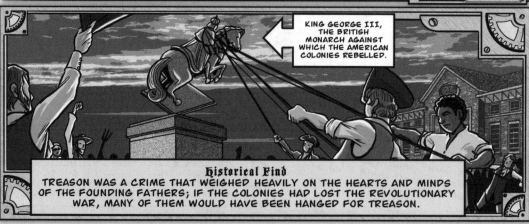

KING GEORGE III, THE BRITISH MONARCH AGAINST WHICH THE AMERICAN COLONIES REBELLED.

Historical Find
TREASON WAS A CRIME THAT WEIGHED HEAVILY ON THE HEARTS AND MINDS OF THE FOUNDING FATHERS; IF THE COLONIES HAD LOST THE REVOLUTIONARY WAR, MANY OF THEM WOULD HAVE BEEN HANGED FOR TREASON.

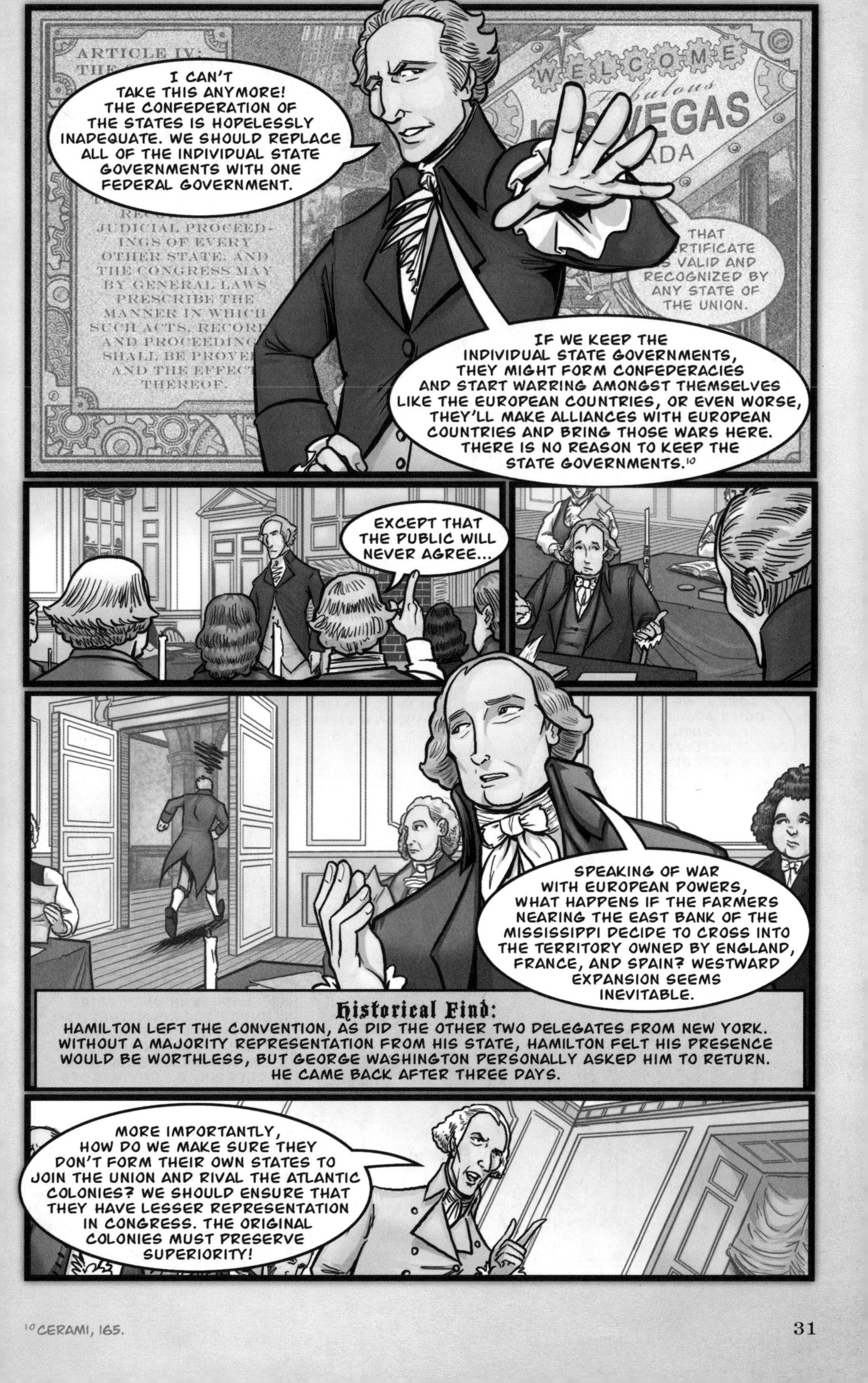
I CAN'T TAKE THIS ANYMORE! THE CONFEDERATION OF THE STATES IS HOPELESSLY INADEQUATE. WE SHOULD REPLACE ALL OF THE INDIVIDUAL STATE GOVERNMENTS WITH ONE FEDERAL GOVERNMENT.
IF WE KEEP THE INDIVIDUAL STATE GOVERNMENTS, THEY MIGHT FORM CONFEDERACIES AND START WARRING AMONGST THEMSELVES LIKE THE EUROPEAN COUNTRIES, OR EVEN WORSE, THEY'LL MAKE ALLIANCES WITH EUROPEAN COUNTRIES AND BRING THOSE WARS HERE. THERE IS NO REASON TO KEEP THE STATE GOVERNMENTS.[10]
EXCEPT THAT THE PUBLIC WILL NEVER AGREE...
SPEAKING OF WAR WITH EUROPEAN POWERS, WHAT HAPPENS IF THE FARMERS NEARING THE EAST BANK OF THE MISSISSIPPI DECIDE TO CROSS INTO THE TERRITORY OWNED BY ENGLAND, FRANCE, AND SPAIN? WESTWARD EXPANSION SEEMS INEVITABLE.
Historical Find:
HAMILTON LEFT THE CONVENTION, AS DID THE OTHER TWO DELEGATES FROM NEW YORK. WITHOUT A MAJORITY REPRESENTATION FROM HIS STATE, HAMILTON FELT HIS PRESENCE WOULD BE WORTHLESS, BUT GEORGE WASHINGTON PERSONALLY ASKED HIM TO RETURN. HE CAME BACK AFTER THREE DAYS.
MORE IMPORTANTLY, HOW DO WE MAKE SURE THEY DON'T FORM THEIR OWN STATES TO JOIN THE UNION AND RIVAL THE ATLANTIC COLONIES? WE SHOULD ENSURE THAT THEY HAVE LESSER REPRESENTATION IN CONGRESS. THE ORIGINAL COLONIES MUST PRESERVE SUPERIORITY!

[10] CERAMI, 165.

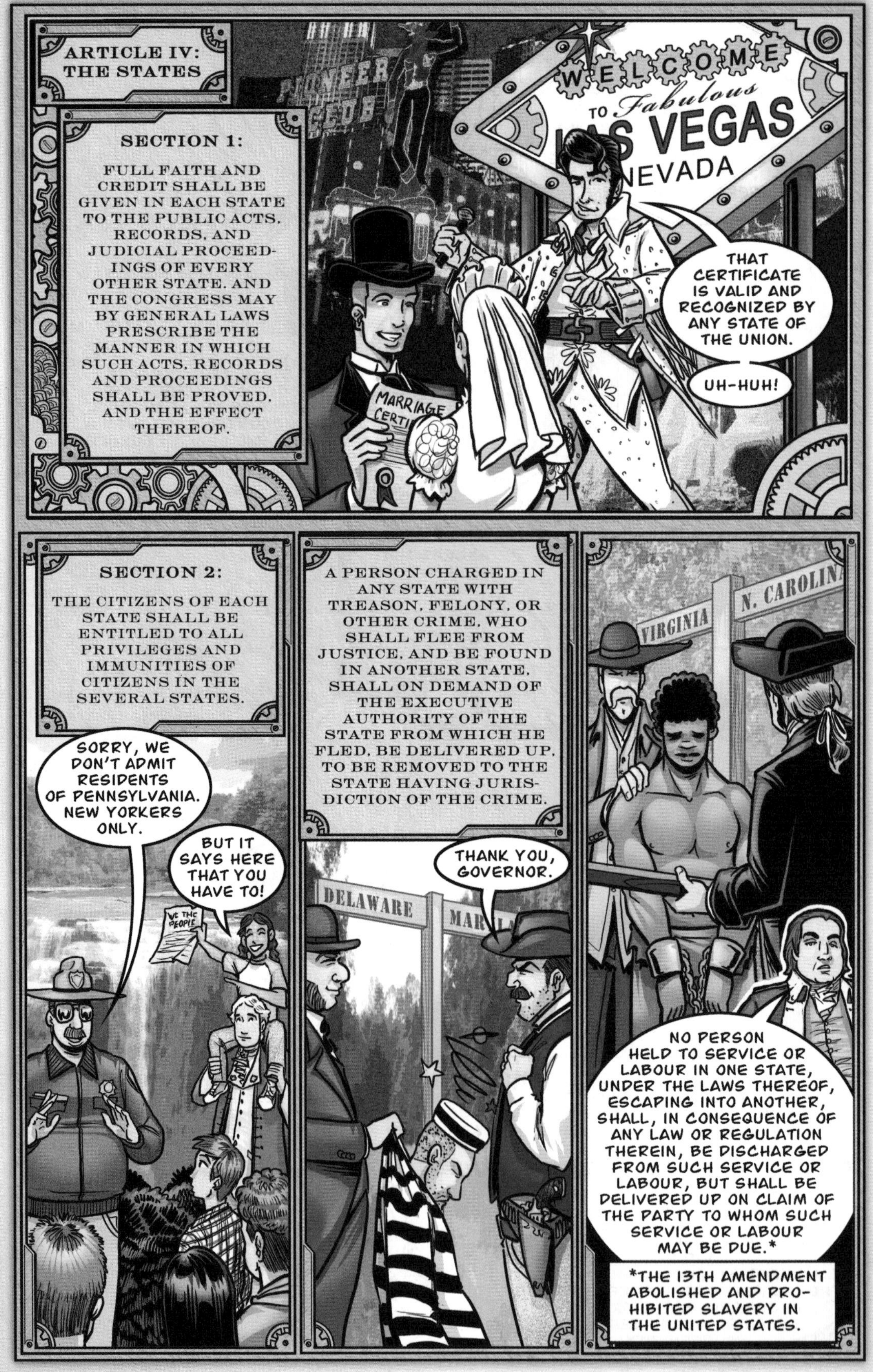
ARTICLE IV: THE STATES
SECTION 1:
FULL FAITH AND CREDIT SHALL BE GIVEN IN EACH STATE TO THE PUBLIC ACTS, RECORDS, AND JUDICIAL PROCEEDINGS OF EVERY OTHER STATE. AND THE CONGRESS MAY BY GENERAL LAWS PRESCRIBE THE MANNER IN WHICH SUCH ACTS, RECORDS AND PROCEEDINGS SHALL BE PROVED, AND THE EFFECT THEREOF.
WELCOME TO Fabulous LAS VEGAS NEVADA
MARRIAGE CERTI
THAT CERTIFICATE IS VALID AND RECOGNIZED BY ANY STATE OF THE UNION.
UH-HUH!
SECTION 2:
THE CITIZENS OF EACH STATE SHALL BE ENTITLED TO ALL PRIVILEGES AND IMMUNITIES OF CITIZENS IN THE SEVERAL STATES.
SORRY, WE DON'T ADMIT RESIDENTS OF PENNSYLVANIA. NEW YORKERS ONLY.
BUT IT SAYS HERE THAT YOU HAVE TO!
WE THE PEOPLE
A PERSON CHARGED IN ANY STATE WITH TREASON, FELONY, OR OTHER CRIME, WHO SHALL FLEE FROM JUSTICE, AND BE FOUND IN ANOTHER STATE, SHALL ON DEMAND OF THE EXECUTIVE AUTHORITY OF THE STATE FROM WHICH HE FLED, BE DELIVERED UP, TO BE REMOVED TO THE STATE HAVING JURISDICTION OF THE CRIME.
THANK YOU, GOVERNOR.
DELAWARE
VIRGINIA
N. CAROLINA
NO PERSON HELD TO SERVICE OR LABOUR IN ONE STATE, UNDER THE LAWS THEREOF, ESCAPING INTO ANOTHER, SHALL, IN CONSEQUENCE OF ANY LAW OR REGULATION THEREIN, BE DISCHARGED FROM SUCH SERVICE OR LABOUR, BUT SHALL BE DELIVERED UP ON CLAIM OF THE PARTY TO WHOM SUCH SERVICE OR LABOUR MAY BE DUE.*
*THE 13TH AMENDMENT ABOLISHED AND PROHIBITED SLAVERY IN THE UNITED STATES.

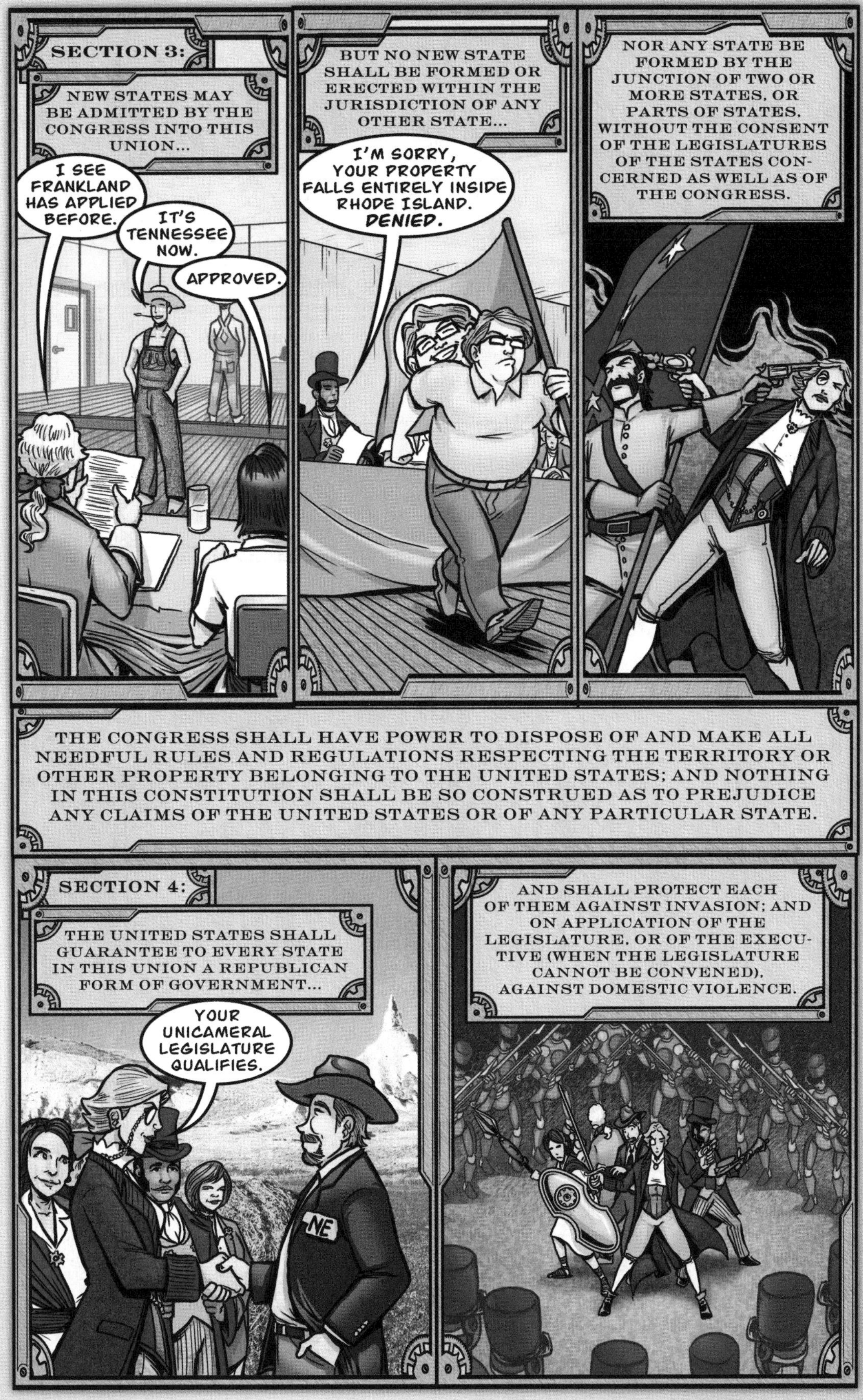
SECTION 3:
NEW STATES MAY BE ADMITTED BY THE CONGRESS INTO THIS UNION...
I SEE FRANKLAND HAS APPLIED BEFORE.
IT'S TENNESSEE NOW.
APPROVED.
BUT NO NEW STATE SHALL BE FORMED OR ERECTED WITHIN THE JURISDICTION OF ANY OTHER STATE...
I'M SORRY, YOUR PROPERTY FALLS ENTIRELY INSIDE RHODE ISLAND. DENIED.
NOR ANY STATE BE FORMED BY THE JUNCTION OF TWO OR MORE STATES, OR PARTS OF STATES, WITHOUT THE CONSENT OF THE LEGISLATURES OF THE STATES CONCERNED AS WELL AS OF THE CONGRESS.
THE CONGRESS SHALL HAVE POWER TO DISPOSE OF AND MAKE ALL NEEDFUL RULES AND REGULATIONS RESPECTING THE TERRITORY OR OTHER PROPERTY BELONGING TO THE UNITED STATES; AND NOTHING IN THIS CONSTITUTION SHALL BE SO CONSTRUED AS TO PREJUDICE ANY CLAIMS OF THE UNITED STATES OR OF ANY PARTICULAR STATE.
SECTION 4:
THE UNITED STATES SHALL GUARANTEE TO EVERY STATE IN THIS UNION A REPUBLICAN FORM OF GOVERNMENT...
YOUR UNICAMERAL LEGISLATURE QUALIFIES.
NE
AND SHALL PROTECT EACH OF THEM AGAINST INVASION; AND ON APPLICATION OF THE LEGISLATURE, OR OF THE EXECUTIVE (WHEN THE LEGISLATURE CANNOT BE CONVENED), AGAINST DOMESTIC VIOLENCE.

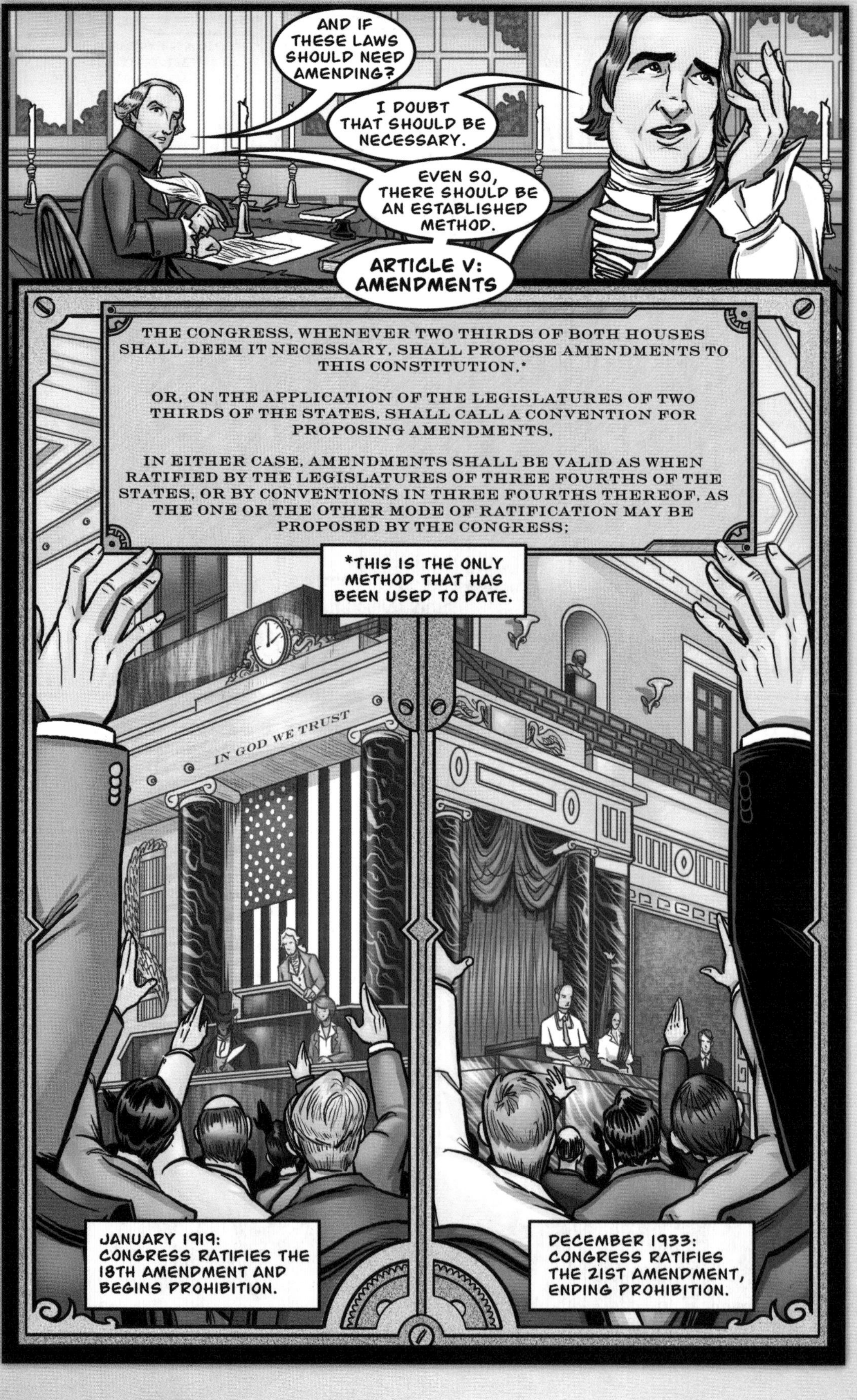
AND IF THESE LAWS SHOULD NEED AMENDING?
I DOUBT THAT SHOULD BE NECESSARY.
EVEN SO, THERE SHOULD BE AN ESTABLISHED METHOD.
ARTICLE V: AMENDMENTS
THE CONGRESS, WHENEVER TWO THIRDS OF BOTH HOUSES SHALL DEEM IT NECESSARY, SHALL PROPOSE AMENDMENTS TO THIS CONSTITUTION,*
OR, ON THE APPLICATION OF THE LEGISLATURES OF TWO THIRDS OF THE STATES, SHALL CALL A CONVENTION FOR PROPOSING AMENDMENTS,
IN EITHER CASE, AMENDMENTS SHALL BE VALID AS WHEN RATIFIED BY THE LEGISLATURES OF THREE FOURTHS OF THE STATES, OR BY CONVENTIONS IN THREE FOURTHS THEREOF, AS THE ONE OR THE OTHER MODE OF RATIFICATION MAY BE PROPOSED BY THE CONGRESS;
*THIS IS THE ONLY METHOD THAT HAS BEEN USED TO DATE.
IN GOD WE TRUST
JANUARY 1919: CONGRESS RATIFIES THE 18TH AMENDMENT AND BEGINS PROHIBITION.
DECEMBER 1933: CONGRESS RATIFIES THE 21ST AMENDMENT, ENDING PROHIBITION.

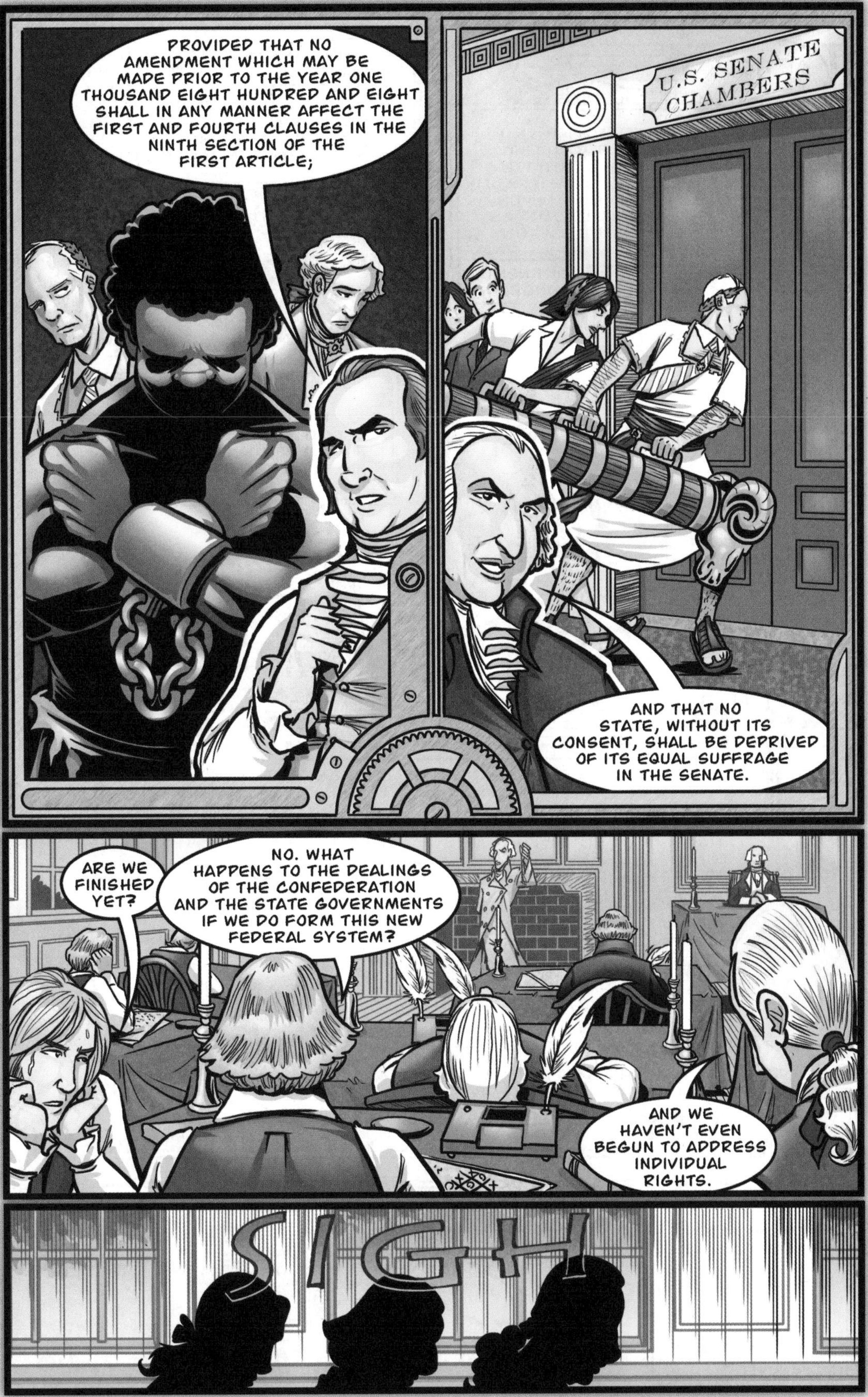
PROVIDED THAT NO AMENDMENT WHICH MAY BE MADE PRIOR TO THE YEAR ONE THOUSAND EIGHT HUNDRED AND EIGHT SHALL IN ANY MANNER AFFECT THE FIRST AND FOURTH CLAUSES IN THE NINTH SECTION OF THE FIRST ARTICLE;
U.S. SENATE CHAMBERS
AND THAT NO STATE, WITHOUT ITS CONSENT, SHALL BE DEPRIVED OF ITS EQUAL SUFFRAGE IN THE SENATE.
ARE WE FINISHED YET?
NO. WHAT HAPPENS TO THE DEALINGS OF THE CONFEDERATION AND THE STATE GOVERNMENTS IF WE DO FORM THIS NEW FEDERAL SYSTEM?
AND WE HAVEN'T EVEN BEGUN TO ADDRESS INDIVIDUAL RIGHTS.
SIGH

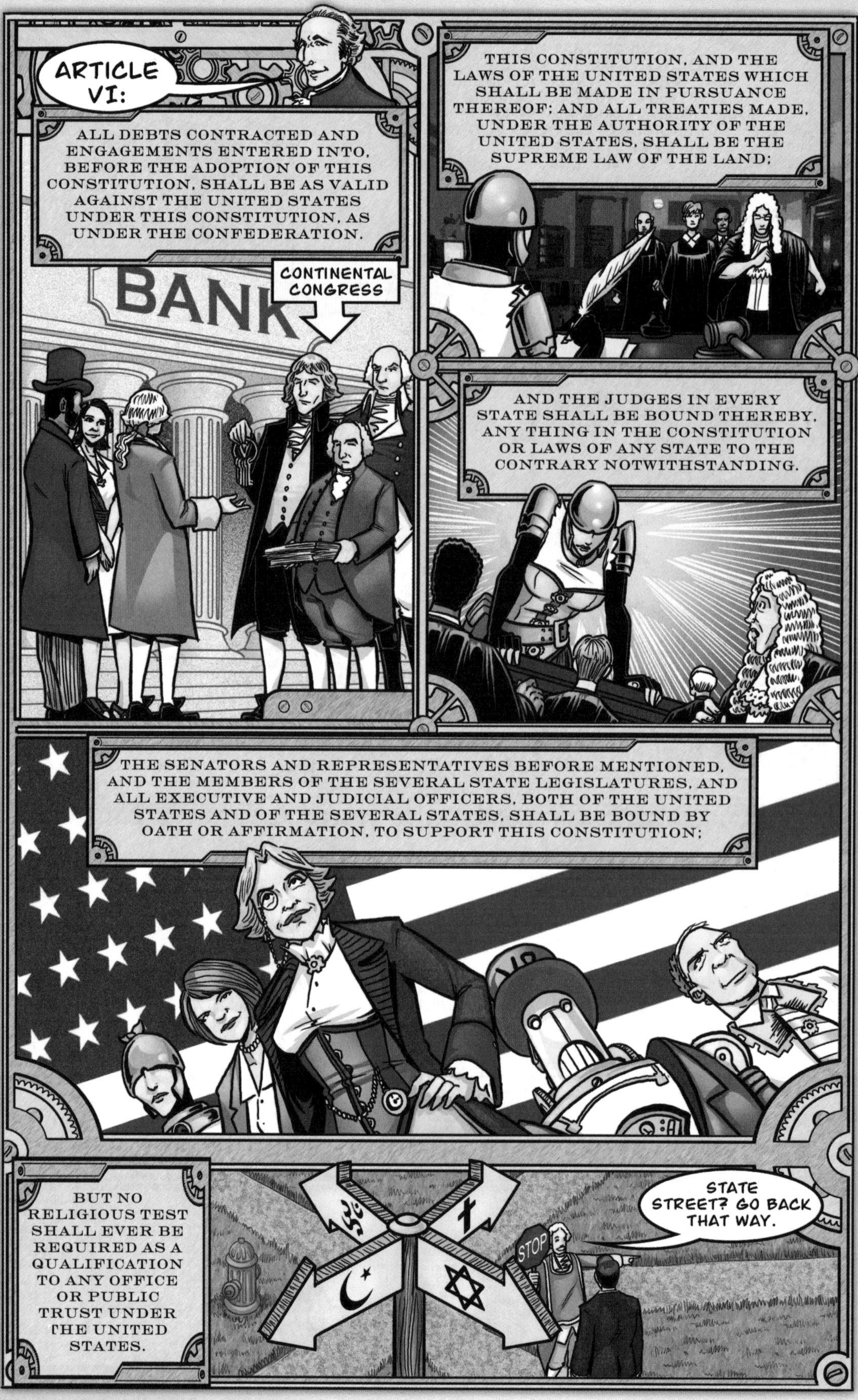
ARTICLE VI:
ALL DEBTS CONTRACTED AND ENGAGEMENTS ENTERED INTO, BEFORE THE ADOPTION OF THIS CONSTITUTION, SHALL BE AS VALID AGAINST THE UNITED STATES UNDER THIS CONSTITUTION, AS UNDER THE CONFEDERATION.
BANK
CONTINENTAL CONGRESS
THIS CONSTITUTION, AND THE LAWS OF THE UNITED STATES WHICH SHALL BE MADE IN PURSUANCE THEREOF; AND ALL TREATIES MADE, UNDER THE AUTHORITY OF THE UNITED STATES, SHALL BE THE SUPREME LAW OF THE LAND;
AND THE JUDGES IN EVERY STATE SHALL BE BOUND THEREBY, ANY THING IN THE CONSTITUTION OR LAWS OF ANY STATE TO THE CONTRARY NOTWITHSTANDING.
THE SENATORS AND REPRESENTATIVES BEFORE MENTIONED, AND THE MEMBERS OF THE SEVERAL STATE LEGISLATURES, AND ALL EXECUTIVE AND JUDICIAL OFFICERS, BOTH OF THE UNITED STATES AND OF THE SEVERAL STATES, SHALL BE BOUND BY OATH OR AFFIRMATION, TO SUPPORT THIS CONSTITUTION;
BUT NO RELIGIOUS TEST SHALL EVER BE REQUIRED AS A QUALIFICATION TO ANY OFFICE OR PUBLIC TRUST UNDER THE UNITED STATES.
STOP
STATE STREET? GO BACK THAT WAY.

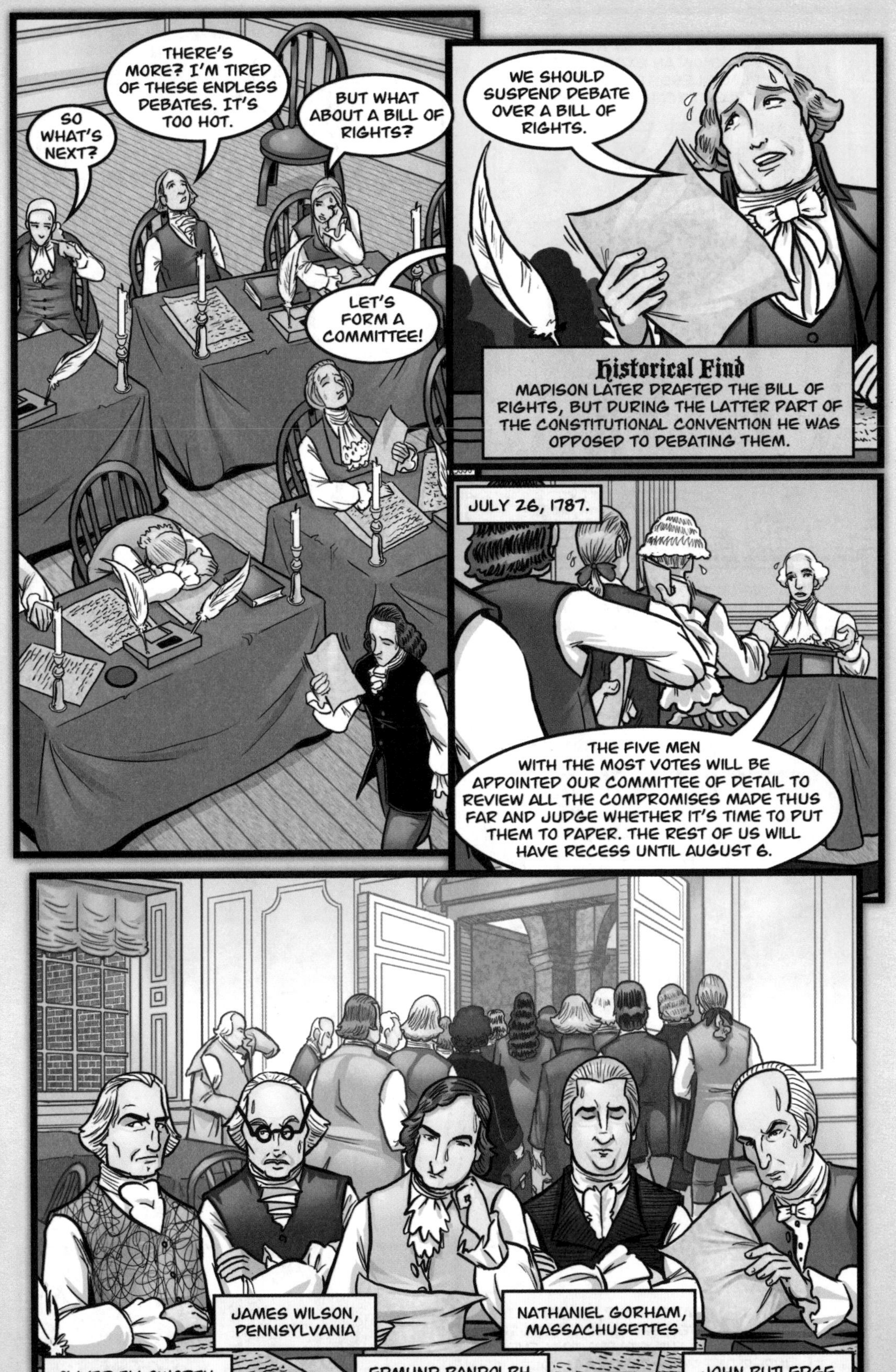
SO WHAT'S NEXT?
THERE'S MORE? I'M TIRED OF THESE ENDLESS DEBATES. IT'S TOO HOT.
BUT WHAT ABOUT A BILL OF RIGHTS?
LET'S FORM A COMMITTEE!
WE SHOULD SUSPEND DEBATE OVER A BILL OF RIGHTS.
Historical Find
MADISON LATER DRAFTED THE BILL OF RIGHTS, BUT DURING THE LATTER PART OF THE CONSTITUTIONAL CONVENTION HE WAS OPPOSED TO DEBATING THEM.
JULY 26, 1787.
THE FIVE MEN WITH THE MOST VOTES WILL BE APPOINTED OUR COMMITTEE OF DETAIL TO REVIEW ALL THE COMPROMISES MADE THUS FAR AND JUDGE WHETHER IT'S TIME TO PUT THEM TO PAPER. THE REST OF US WILL HAVE RECESS UNTIL AUGUST 6.
OLIVER ELLSWORTH, CONNECTICUT
JAMES WILSON, PENNSYLVANIA
EDMUND RANDOLPH, VIRGINIA
NATHANIEL GORHAM, MASSACHUSETTES
JOHN RUTLEDGE, SOUTH CAROLINA

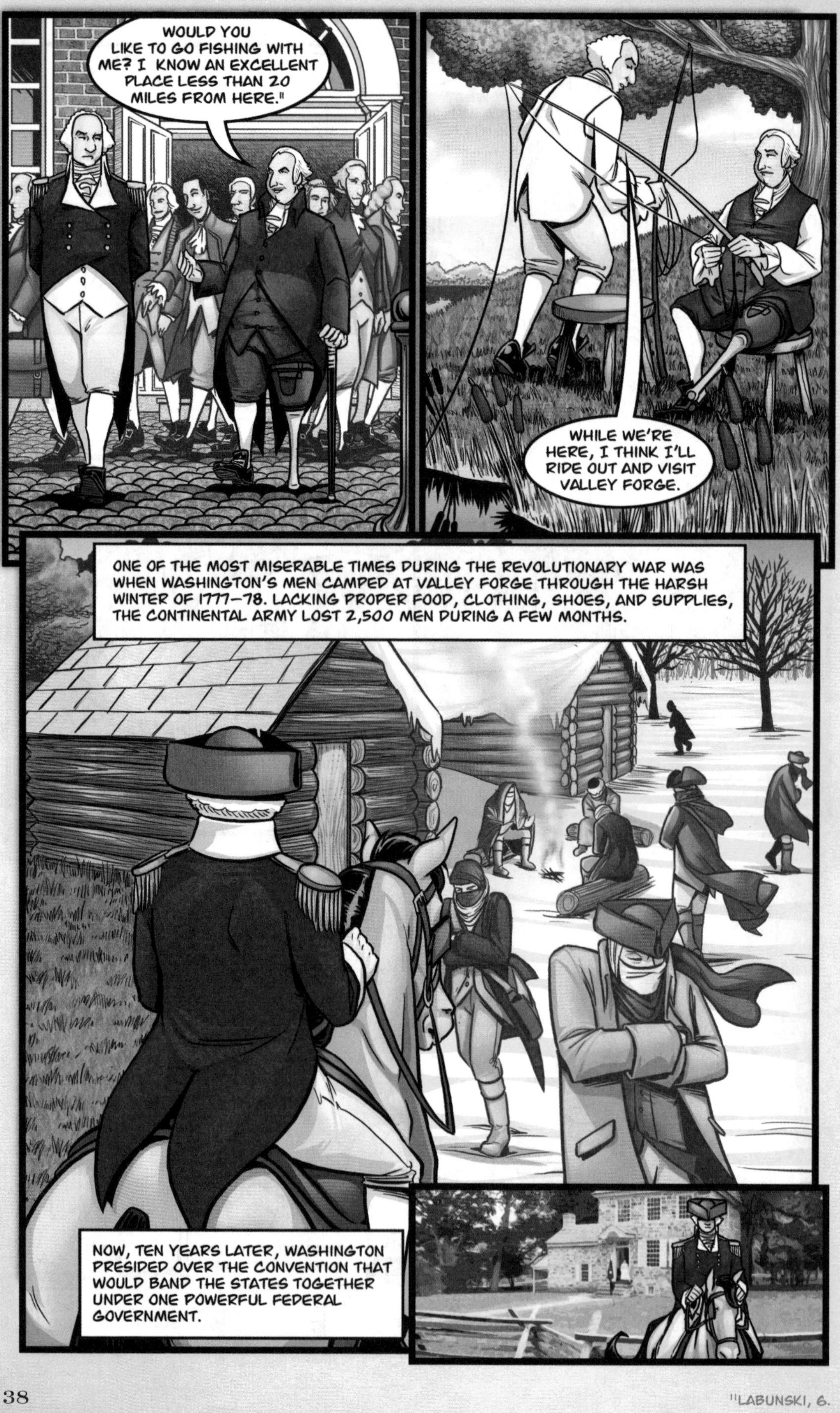
WOULD YOU LIKE TO GO FISHING WITH ME? I KNOW AN EXCELLENT PLACE LESS THAN 20 MILES FROM HERE."
WHILE WE'RE HERE, I THINK I'LL RIDE OUT AND VISIT VALLEY FORGE.
ONE OF THE MOST MISERABLE TIMES DURING THE REVOLUTIONARY WAR WAS WHEN WASHINGTON'S MEN CAMPED AT VALLEY FORGE THROUGH THE HARSH WINTER OF 1777–78. LACKING PROPER FOOD, CLOTHING, SHOES, AND SUPPLIES, THE CONTINENTAL ARMY LOST 2,500 MEN DURING A FEW MONTHS.
NOW, TEN YEARS LATER, WASHINGTON PRESIDED OVER THE CONVENTION THAT WOULD BAND THE STATES TOGETHER UNDER ONE POWERFUL FEDERAL GOVERNMENT.

"LABUNSKI, 6.

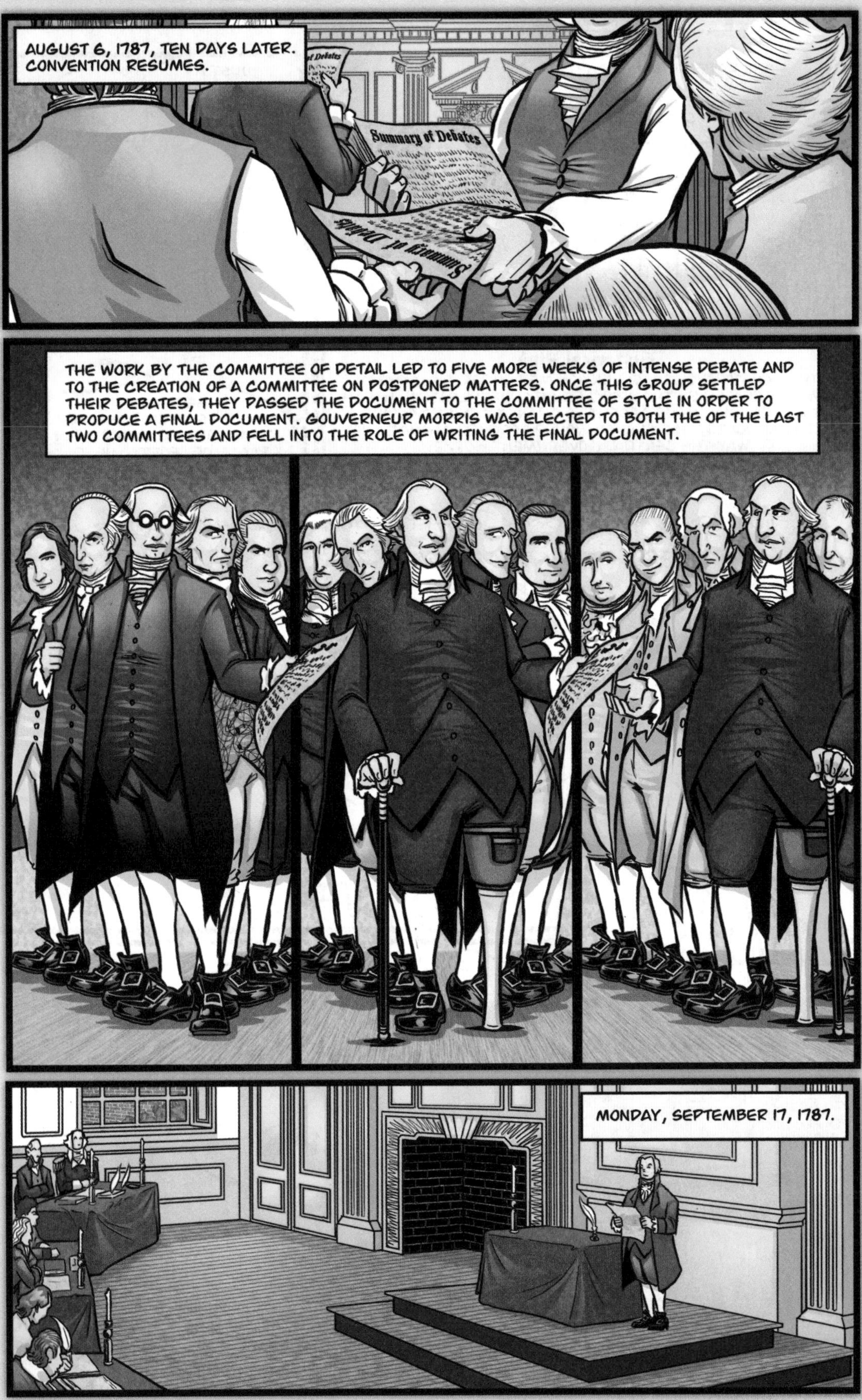
AUGUST 6, 1787, TEN DAYS LATER. CONVENTION RESUMES.
Summary of Debates
THE WORK BY THE COMMITTEE OF DETAIL LED TO FIVE MORE WEEKS OF INTENSE DEBATE AND TO THE CREATION OF A COMMITTEE ON POSTPONED MATTERS. ONCE THIS GROUP SETTLED THEIR DEBATES, THEY PASSED THE DOCUMENT TO THE COMMITTEE OF STYLE IN ORDER TO PRODUCE A FINAL DOCUMENT. GOUVERNEUR MORRIS WAS ELECTED TO BOTH THE OF THE LAST TWO COMMITTEES AND FELL INTO THE ROLE OF WRITING THE FINAL DOCUMENT.
MONDAY, SEPTEMBER 17, 1787.

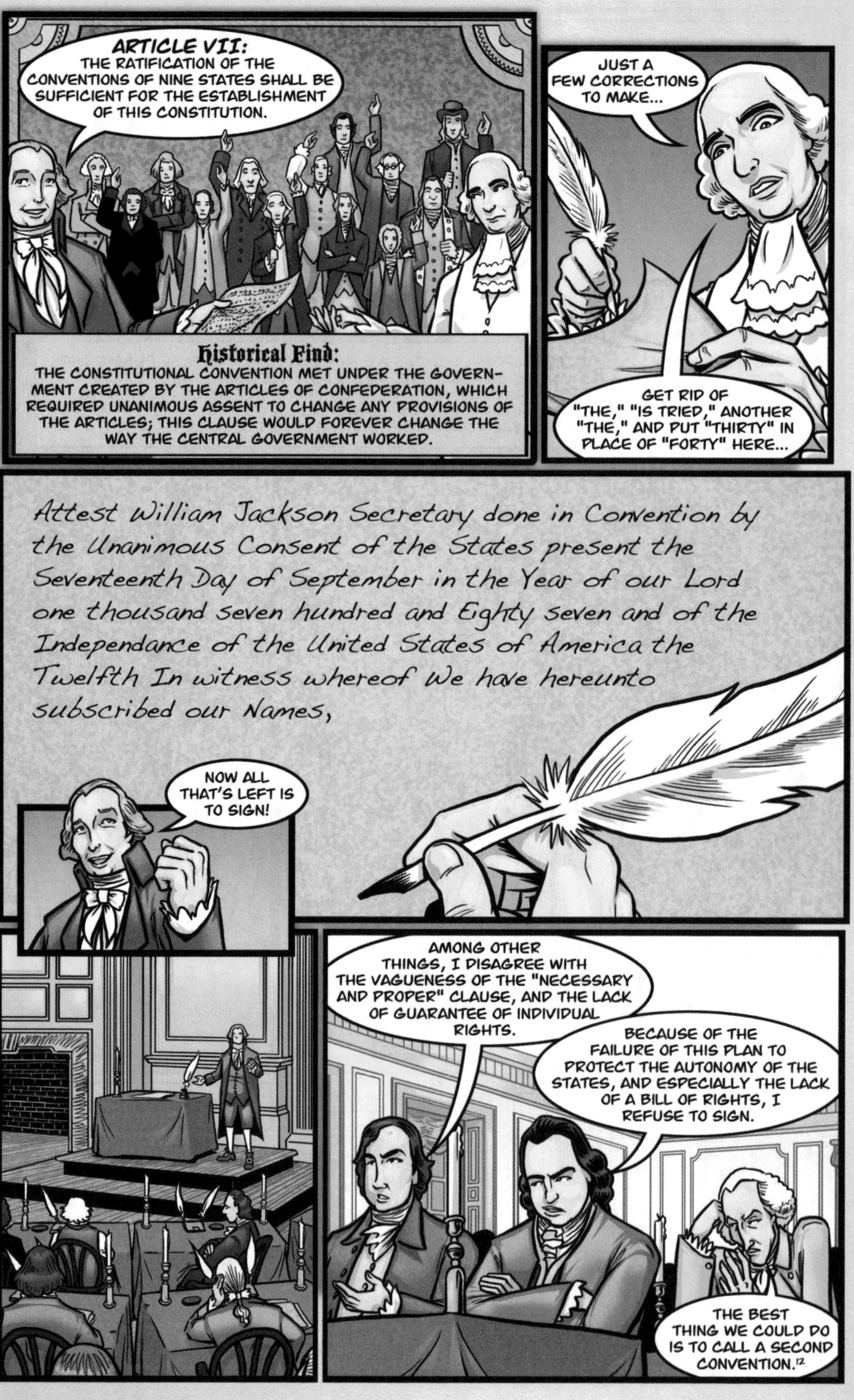
ARTICLE VII:
THE RATIFICATION OF THE CONVENTIONS OF NINE STATES SHALL BE SUFFICIENT FOR THE ESTABLISHMENT OF THIS CONSTITUTION.
Historical Find:
THE CONSTITUTIONAL CONVENTION MET UNDER THE GOVERNMENT CREATED BY THE ARTICLES OF CONFEDERATION, WHICH REQUIRED UNANIMOUS ASSENT TO CHANGE ANY PROVISIONS OF THE ARTICLES; THIS CLAUSE WOULD FOREVER CHANGE THE WAY THE CENTRAL GOVERNMENT WORKED.
JUST A FEW CORRECTIONS TO MAKE...
GET RID OF "THE," "IS TRIED," ANOTHER "THE," AND PUT "THIRTY" IN PLACE OF "FORTY" HERE...
Attest William Jackson Secretary done in Convention by the Unanimous Consent of the States present the Seventeenth Day of September in the Year of our Lord one thousand seven hundred and Eighty seven and of the Independance of the United States of America the Twelfth In witness whereof We have hereunto subscribed our Names,
NOW ALL THAT'S LEFT IS TO SIGN!
AMONG OTHER THINGS, I DISAGREE WITH THE VAGUENESS OF THE "NECESSARY AND PROPER" CLAUSE, AND THE LACK OF GUARANTEE OF INDIVIDUAL RIGHTS.
BECAUSE OF THE FAILURE OF THIS PLAN TO PROTECT THE AUTONOMY OF THE STATES, AND ESPECIALLY THE LACK OF A BILL OF RIGHTS, I REFUSE TO SIGN.
THE BEST THING WE COULD DO IS TO CALL A SECOND CONVENTION.[12]

[12] LABUNSKI, 8-12.

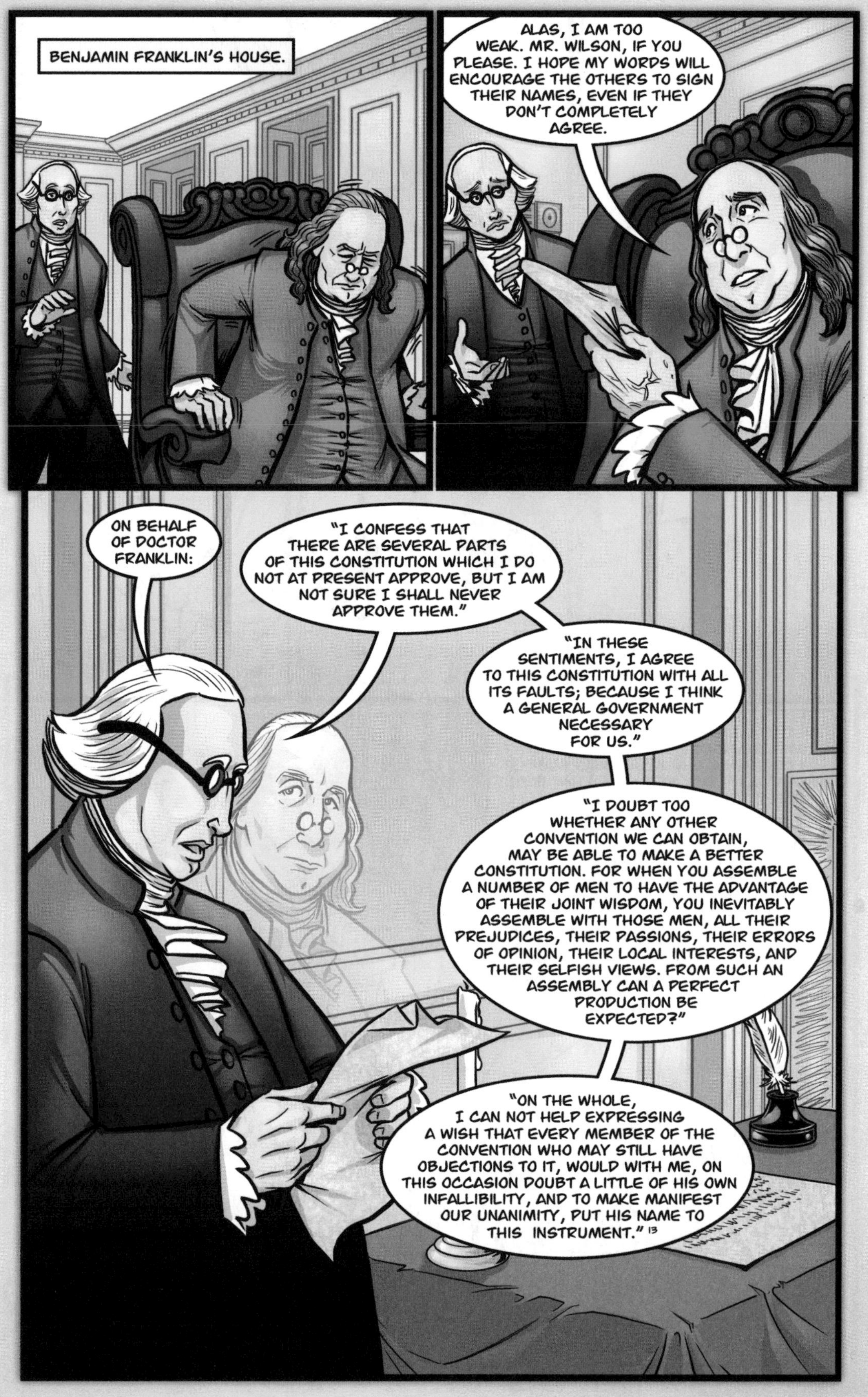
BENJAMIN FRANKLIN'S HOUSE.
ALAS, I AM TOO WEAK. MR. WILSON, IF YOU PLEASE. I HOPE MY WORDS WILL ENCOURAGE THE OTHERS TO SIGN THEIR NAMES, EVEN IF THEY DON'T COMPLETELY AGREE.
ON BEHALF OF DOCTOR FRANKLIN:
"I CONFESS THAT THERE ARE SEVERAL PARTS OF THIS CONSTITUTION WHICH I DO NOT AT PRESENT APPROVE, BUT I AM NOT SURE I SHALL NEVER APPROVE THEM."
"IN THESE SENTIMENTS, I AGREE TO THIS CONSTITUTION WITH ALL ITS FAULTS; BECAUSE I THINK A GENERAL GOVERNMENT NECESSARY FOR US."
"I DOUBT TOO WHETHER ANY OTHER CONVENTION WE CAN OBTAIN, MAY BE ABLE TO MAKE A BETTER CONSTITUTION. FOR WHEN YOU ASSEMBLE A NUMBER OF MEN TO HAVE THE ADVANTAGE OF THEIR JOINT WISDOM, YOU INEVITABLY ASSEMBLE WITH THOSE MEN, ALL THEIR PREJUDICES, THEIR PASSIONS, THEIR ERRORS OF OPINION, THEIR LOCAL INTERESTS, AND THEIR SELFISH VIEWS. FROM SUCH AN ASSEMBLY CAN A PERFECT PRODUCTION BE EXPECTED?"
"ON THE WHOLE, I CAN NOT HELP EXPRESSING A WISH THAT EVERY MEMBER OF THE CONVENTION WHO MAY STILL HAVE OBJECTIONS TO IT, WOULD WITH ME, ON THIS OCCASION DOUBT A LITTLE OF HIS OWN INFALLIBILITY, AND TO MAKE MANIFEST OUR UNANIMITY, PUT HIS NAME TO THIS INSTRUMENT."[13]

[13] RALPH KETCHAM, *THE ANTI-FEDERALIST PAPERS AND THE CONSTITUTIONAL CONVENTION DEBATES* (NEW YORK: SIGNET CLASSICS, 2003), 177.

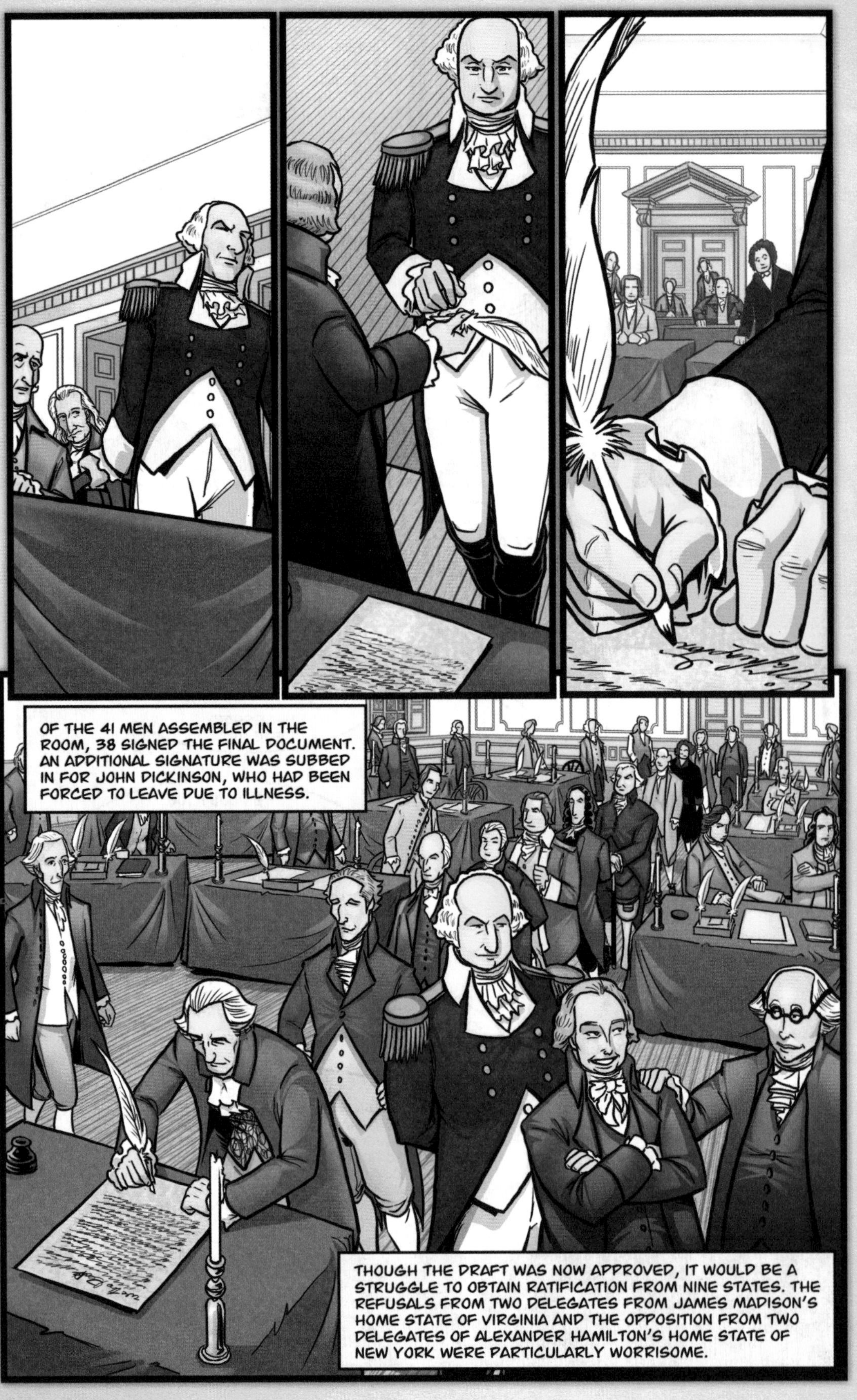
OF THE 41 MEN ASSEMBLED IN THE ROOM, 38 SIGNED THE FINAL DOCUMENT. AN ADDITIONAL SIGNATURE WAS SUBBED IN FOR JOHN DICKINSON, WHO HAD BEEN FORCED TO LEAVE DUE TO ILLNESS.
THOUGH THE DRAFT WAS NOW APPROVED, IT WOULD BE A STRUGGLE TO OBTAIN RATIFICATION FROM NINE STATES. THE REFUSALS FROM TWO DELEGATES FROM JAMES MADISON'S HOME STATE OF VIRGINIA AND THE OPPOSITION FROM TWO DELEGATES OF ALEXANDER HAMILTON'S HOME STATE OF NEW YORK WERE PARTICULARLY WORRISOME.

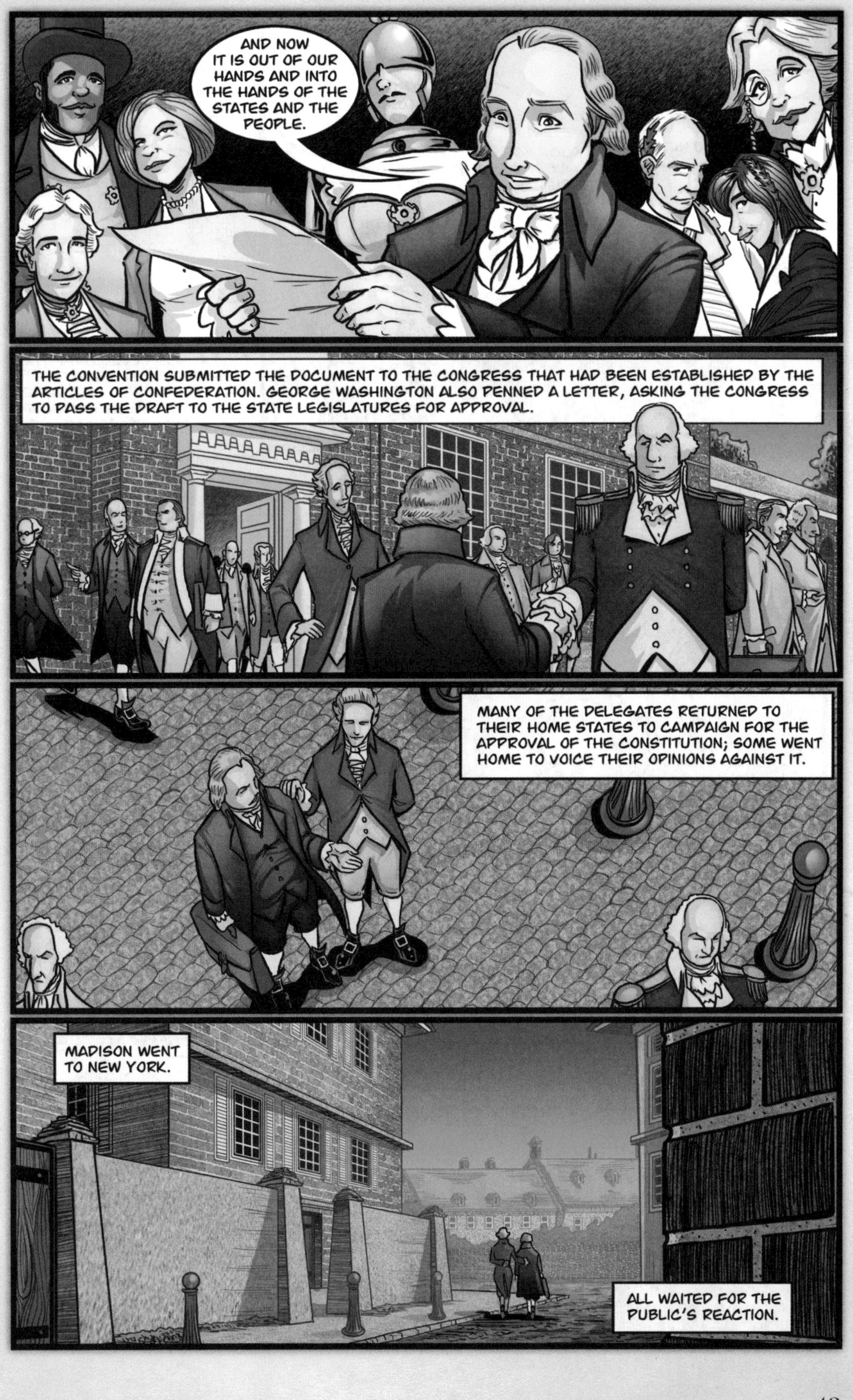
AND NOW IT IS OUT OF OUR HANDS AND INTO THE HANDS OF THE STATES AND THE PEOPLE.
THE CONVENTION SUBMITTED THE DOCUMENT TO THE CONGRESS THAT HAD BEEN ESTABLISHED BY THE ARTICLES OF CONFEDERATION. GEORGE WASHINGTON ALSO PENNED A LETTER, ASKING THE CONGRESS TO PASS THE DRAFT TO THE STATE LEGISLATURES FOR APPROVAL.
MANY OF THE DELEGATES RETURNED TO THEIR HOME STATES TO CAMPAIGN FOR THE APPROVAL OF THE CONSTITUTION; SOME WENT HOME TO VOICE THEIR OPINIONS AGAINST IT.
MADISON WENT TO NEW YORK.
ALL WAITED FOR THE PUBLIC'S REACTION.

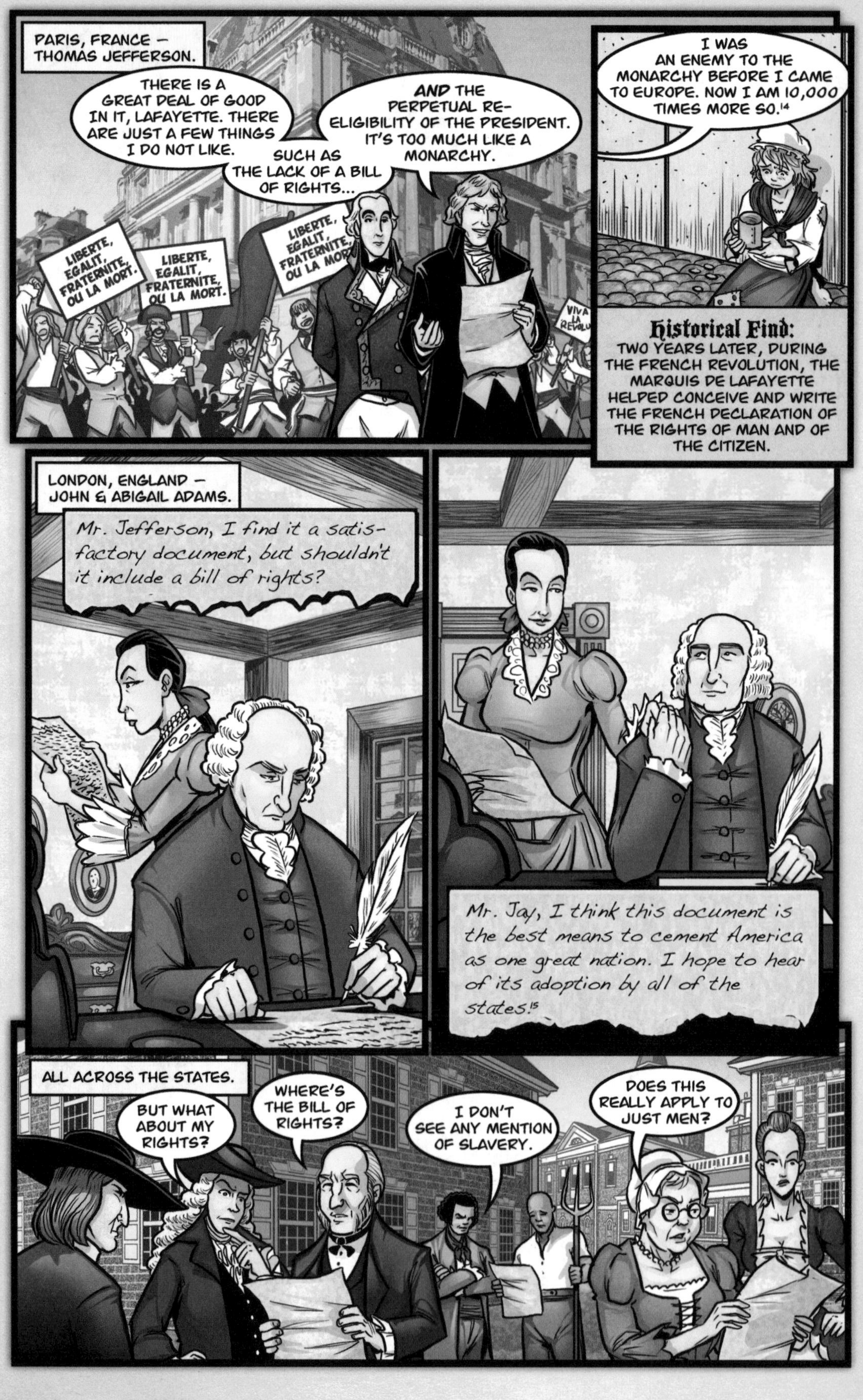

PARIS, FRANCE — THOMAS JEFFERSON.
THERE IS A GREAT DEAL OF GOOD IN IT, LAFAYETTE. THERE ARE JUST A FEW THINGS I DO NOT LIKE.
SUCH AS THE LACK OF A BILL OF RIGHTS...
AND THE PERPETUAL RE-ELIGIBILITY OF THE PRESIDENT. IT'S TOO MUCH LIKE A MONARCHY.
LIBERTE, EGALIT, FRATERNITE, OU LA MORT.
LIBERTE, EGALIT, FRATERNITE, OU LA MORT.
LIBERTE, EGALIT, FRATERNITE, OU LA MORT
VIVA LA REVOLU
I WAS AN ENEMY TO THE MONARCHY BEFORE I CAME TO EUROPE. NOW I AM 10,000 TIMES MORE SO.[14]
Historical Find:
TWO YEARS LATER, DURING THE FRENCH REVOLUTION, THE MARQUIS DE LAFAYETTE HELPED CONCEIVE AND WRITE THE FRENCH DECLARATION OF THE RIGHTS OF MAN AND OF THE CITIZEN.
LONDON, ENGLAND — JOHN & ABIGAIL ADAMS.
Mr. Jefferson, I find it a satisfactory document, but shouldn't it include a bill of rights?
Mr. Jay, I think this document is the best means to cement America as one great nation. I hope to hear of its adoption by all of the states![15]
ALL ACROSS THE STATES.
BUT WHAT ABOUT MY RIGHTS?
WHERE'S THE BILL OF RIGHTS?
I DON'T SEE ANY MENTION OF SLAVERY.
DOES THIS REALLY APPLY TO JUST MEN?

[14]ELLIS, 123. [15]DAVID MCCULLOUGH, JOHN ADAMS (NEW YORK: SIMON & SCHUSTER, 2001), 380.

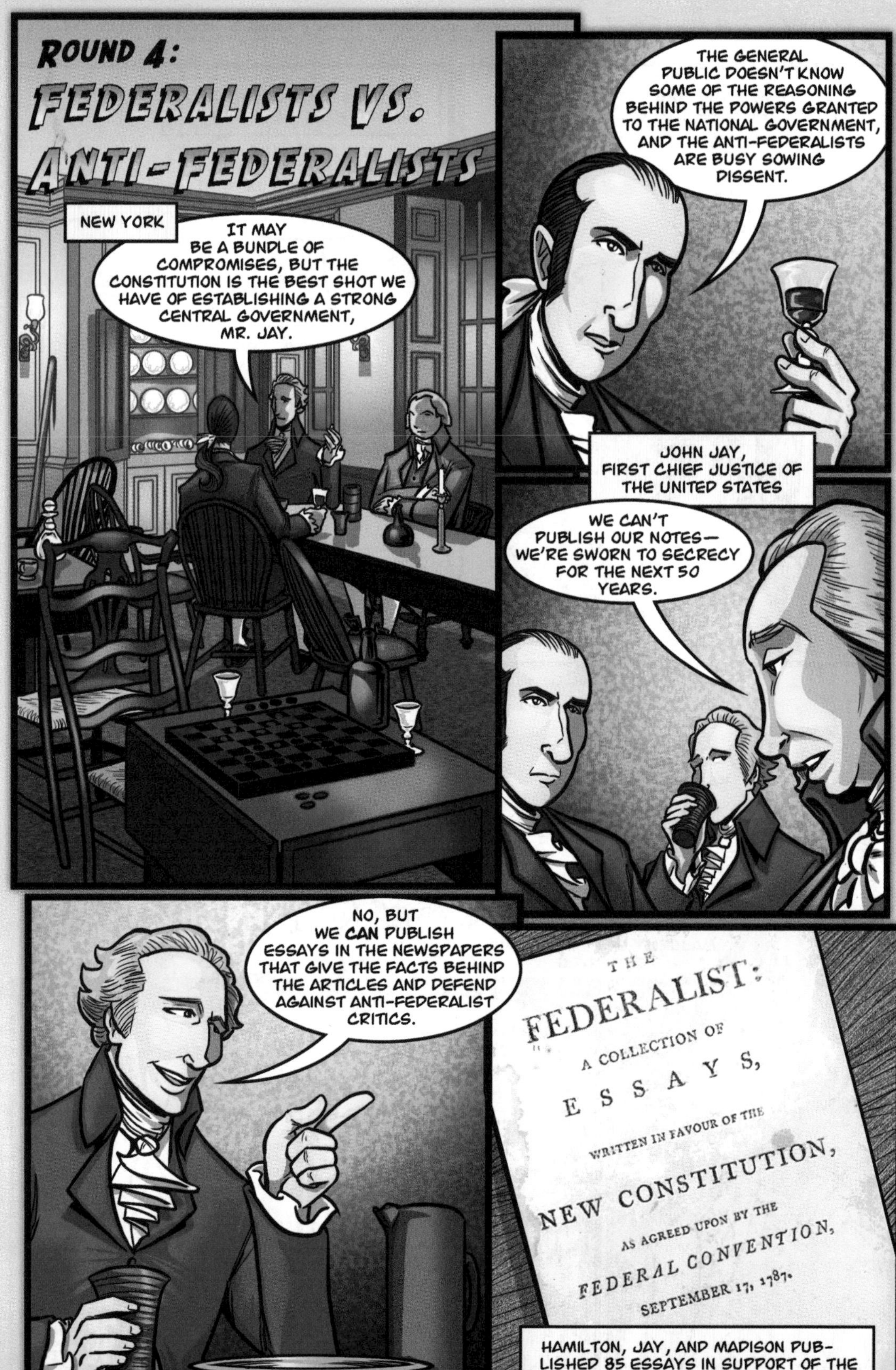
ROUND 4:
FEDERALISTS VS. ANTI-FEDERALISTS
NEW YORK
IT MAY BE A BUNDLE OF COMPROMISES, BUT THE CONSTITUTION IS THE BEST SHOT WE HAVE OF ESTABLISHING A STRONG CENTRAL GOVERNMENT, MR. JAY.
THE GENERAL PUBLIC DOESN'T KNOW SOME OF THE REASONING BEHIND THE POWERS GRANTED TO THE NATIONAL GOVERNMENT, AND THE ANTI-FEDERALISTS ARE BUSY SOWING DISSENT.
JOHN JAY, FIRST CHIEF JUSTICE OF THE UNITED STATES
WE CAN'T PUBLISH OUR NOTES—WE'RE SWORN TO SECRECY FOR THE NEXT 50 YEARS.
NO, BUT WE CAN PUBLISH ESSAYS IN THE NEWSPAPERS THAT GIVE THE FACTS BEHIND THE ARTICLES AND DEFEND AGAINST ANTI-FEDERALIST CRITICS.
THE FEDERALIST: A COLLECTION OF ESSAYS, WRITTEN IN FAVOUR OF THE NEW CONSTITUTION, AS AGREED UPON BY THE FEDERAL CONVENTION, SEPTEMBER 17, 1787.
HAMILTON, JAY, AND MADISON PUBLISHED 85 ESSAYS IN SUPPORT OF THE CONSTITUTION. THESE WERE ORIGINALLY PUBLISHED IN NEWSPAPERS AND LATER BOUND INTO TWO VOLUMES.

IT TOOK TEN MONTHS FOR THE FIRST NINE STATES TO APPROVE THE CONSTITUTION.

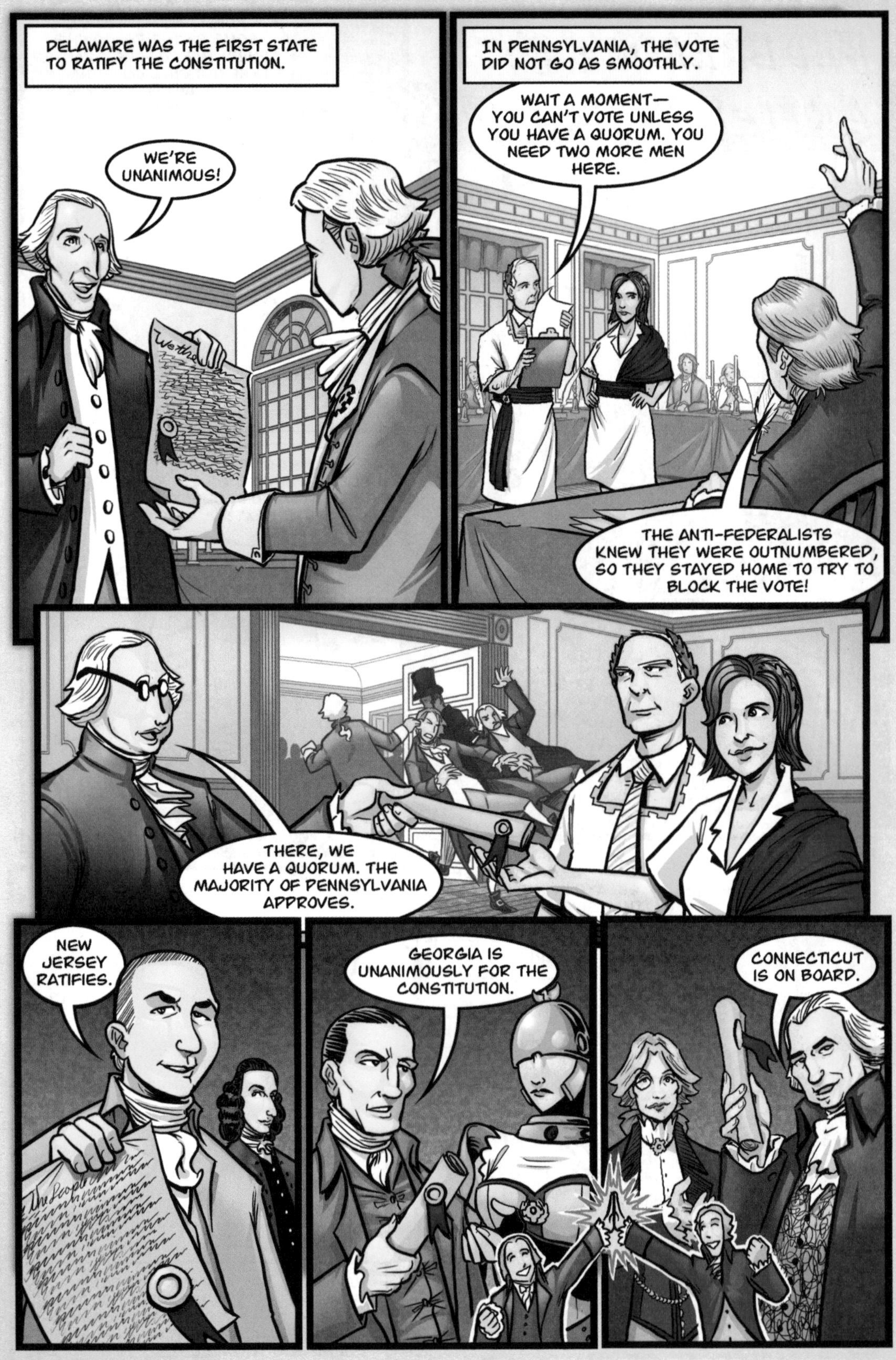

DELAWARE WAS THE FIRST STATE TO RATIFY THE CONSTITUTION.
WE'RE UNANIMOUS!
IN PENNSYLVANIA, THE VOTE DID NOT GO AS SMOOTHLY.
WAIT A MOMENT— YOU CAN'T VOTE UNLESS YOU HAVE A QUORUM. YOU NEED TWO MORE MEN HERE.
THE ANTI-FEDERALISTS KNEW THEY WERE OUTNUMBERED, SO THEY STAYED HOME TO TRY TO BLOCK THE VOTE!
THERE, WE HAVE A QUORUM. THE MAJORITY OF PENNSYLVANIA APPROVES.
NEW JERSEY RATIFIES.
GEORGIA IS UNANIMOUSLY FOR THE CONSTITUTION.
CONNECTICUT IS ON BOARD.

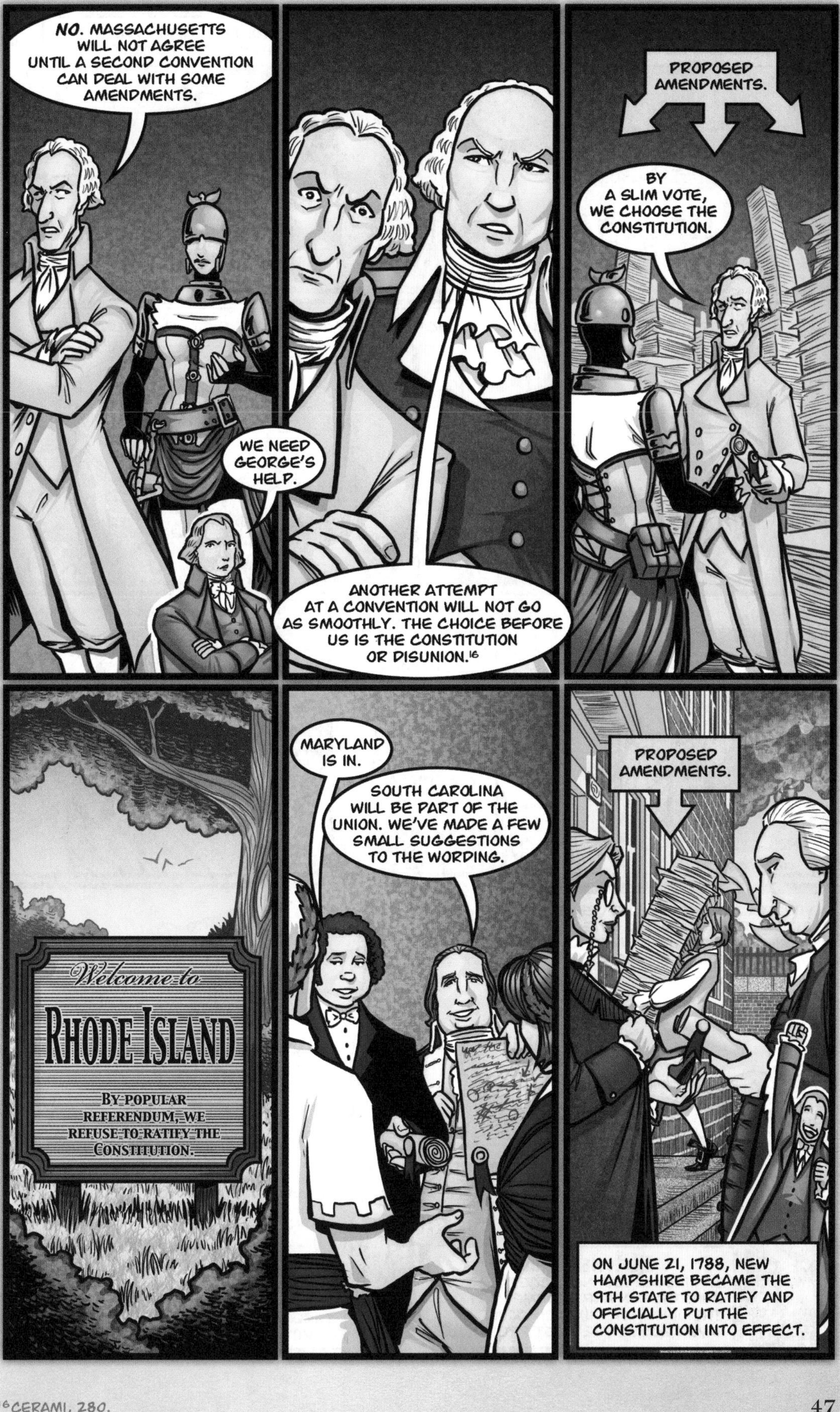
NO. MASSACHUSETTS WILL NOT AGREE UNTIL A SECOND CONVENTION CAN DEAL WITH SOME AMENDMENTS.
WE NEED GEORGE'S HELP.
ANOTHER ATTEMPT AT A CONVENTION WILL NOT GO AS SMOOTHLY. THE CHOICE BEFORE US IS THE CONSTITUTION OR DISUNION.[16]
PROPOSED AMENDMENTS.
BY A SLIM VOTE, WE CHOOSE THE CONSTITUTION.
Welcome to
RHODE ISLAND
BY POPULAR REFERENDUM, WE REFUSE TO RATIFY THE CONSTITUTION.
MARYLAND IS IN.
SOUTH CAROLINA WILL BE PART OF THE UNION. WE'VE MADE A FEW SMALL SUGGESTIONS TO THE WORDING.
PROPOSED AMENDMENTS.
ON JUNE 21, 1788, NEW HAMPSHIRE BECAME THE 9TH STATE TO RATIFY AND OFFICIALLY PUT THE CONSTITUTION INTO EFFECT.

[16] CERAMI, 280.

ALTHOUGH NINE STATES HAD RATIFIED, IT WOULD MEAN LITTLE WITHOUT THE APPROVAL OF THE LARGEST, MOST POPULOUS STATES—ESPECIALLY MADISON AND HAMILTON'S HOME STATES.

EACH ARGUED FOR WEEKS AND WORKED NIGHT AND DAY TO CONVERT THE ANTI-FEDERALISTS.

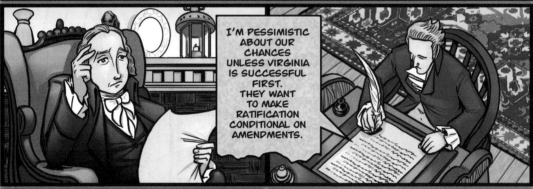

I'M PESSIMISTIC ABOUT OUR CHANCES UNLESS VIRGINIA IS SUCCESSFUL FIRST. THEY WANT TO MAKE RATIFICATION CONDITIONAL ON AMENDMENTS.

VIRGINIA RATIFIED ON JUNE 25, 1788, BY A MARGIN OF ONLY 10 VOTES. MADISON IMMEDIATELY WENT TO WORK DRAFTING A BILL OF RIGHTS.

Historical Find:
IF VIRGINIA HAD NOT ACCEPTED THE CONSTITUTION AND BECOME PART OF THE UNION, WASHINGTON COULD NOT HAVE BECOME THE FIRST PRESIDENT.

THREE WEEKS LATER, NEW YORK VOTED 30 TO 27 TO RATIFY.[17]

[17]CERAMI, 280.

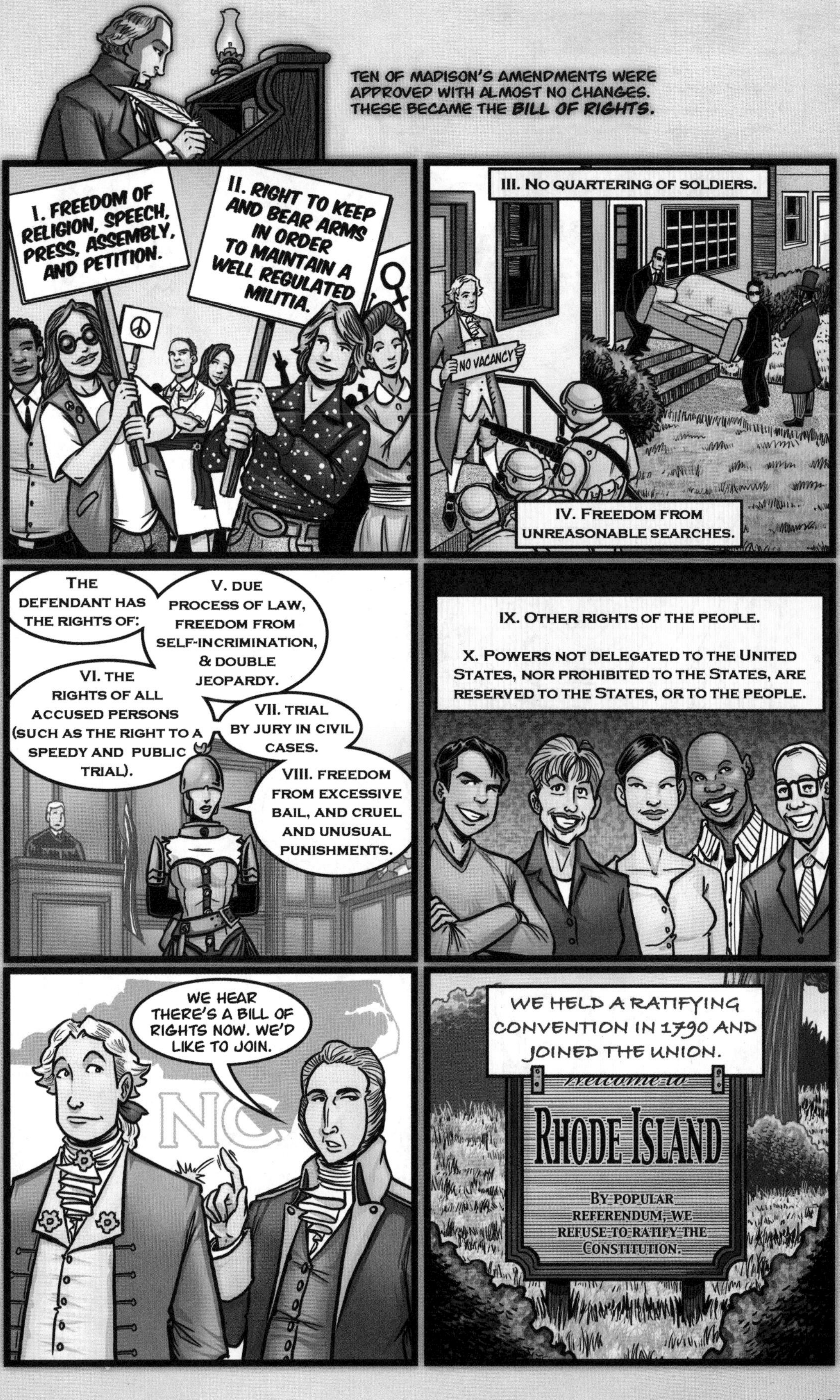
TEN OF MADISON'S AMENDMENTS WERE APPROVED WITH ALMOST NO CHANGES. THESE BECAME THE BILL OF RIGHTS.
I. FREEDOM OF RELIGION, SPEECH, PRESS, ASSEMBLY, AND PETITION.
II. RIGHT TO KEEP AND BEAR ARMS IN ORDER TO MAINTAIN A WELL REGULATED MILITIA.
III. NO QUARTERING OF SOLDIERS.
NO VACANCY
IV. FREEDOM FROM UNREASONABLE SEARCHES.
THE DEFENDANT HAS THE RIGHTS OF:
V. DUE PROCESS OF LAW, FREEDOM FROM SELF-INCRIMINATION, & DOUBLE JEOPARDY.
VI. THE RIGHTS OF ALL ACCUSED PERSONS (SUCH AS THE RIGHT TO A SPEEDY AND PUBLIC TRIAL).
VII. TRIAL BY JURY IN CIVIL CASES.
VIII. FREEDOM FROM EXCESSIVE BAIL, AND CRUEL AND UNUSUAL PUNISHMENTS.
IX. OTHER RIGHTS OF THE PEOPLE.
X. POWERS NOT DELEGATED TO THE UNITED STATES, NOR PROHIBITED TO THE STATES, ARE RESERVED TO THE STATES, OR TO THE PEOPLE.
NC
WE HEAR THERE'S A BILL OF RIGHTS NOW. WE'D LIKE TO JOIN.
WE HELD A RATIFYING CONVENTION IN 1790 AND JOINED THE UNION.
RHODE ISLAND
BY POPULAR REFERENDUM, WE REFUSE TO RATIFY THE CONSTITUTION.

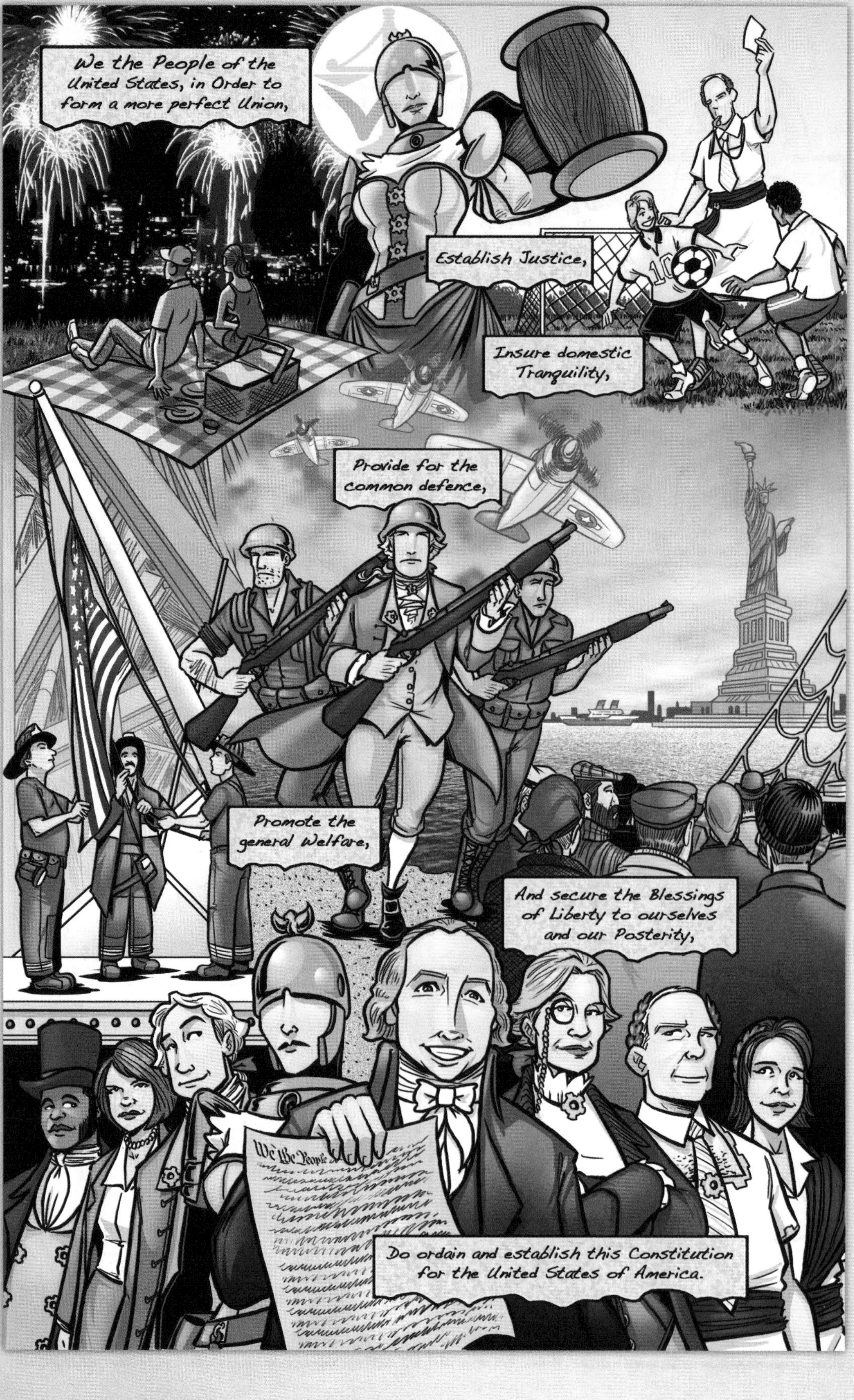
We the People of the United States, in Order to form a more perfect Union,
Establish Justice,
Insure domestic Tranquility,
Provide for the common defence,
Promote the general Welfare,
And secure the Blessings of Liberty to ourselves and our Posterity,
Do ordain and establish this Constitution for the United States of America.

RESOURCES

More information on the founding fathers

HTTP://WWW.ARCHIVES.GOV/EXHIBITS/CHARTERS/CONSTITUTION.HTML

Bibliography of Cited Works

Cerami, Charles. *Young Patriots: The Remarkable Story of Two Men, Their Impossible Plan and the Revolution That Created the Constitution.* Naperville: Sourcebooks, 2005.

Ellis, Joseph J. *American Sphinx: The Character of Thomas Jefferson.* New York: Vintage, 1998.

Ketcham, Ralph. *The Anti-Federalist Papers & The Constitutional Convention Debates.* New York: Signet Classics, 2003.

Labunski, Richard. *James Madison and the Struggle for the Bill of Rights.* New York: Oxford University Press, 2006.

McCullough, David. *John Adams.* New York: Simon & Schuster Paperbacks, 2001.

Other Recommended Reading

Brookhiser, Richard. *Alexander Hamilton, American.* New York: Touchstone, 2000.

Ellis, Joseph J. *Founding Brothers: The Revolutionary Generation.* New York: Vintage, 2002.

Madison, James, Alexander Hamilton, and John Jay. *The Federalist Papers.* New York: Tribeca Books, 2010.

round table companies

About Round Table Companies

Round Table Companies uses a filmmaker's approach to storytelling to inform, educate, and inspire readers. Trusted by *New York Times* bestselling authors Marshall Goldsmith, Chris Anderson, Tony Hsieh, and Robert Cialdini, RTC's approach to creating high quality content eliminates the traditional publishing gatekeepers and allows thought leaders to engage in a fully collaborative team approach to distilling their ideas into either word based or illustrated formats. Whether working with a first time author, or a seasoned veteran, RTC surrounds each author with an entire staff of professionals who understand how to create an emotional and engaging experience for readers.

While 25% of RTC's business is repurposing best-selling non-fiction content in the illustrated form of graphic novels, the company's bread and butter is thought leaders and businesses with powerful messages who either lack the time or the necessary writing skill to articulate their wisdom. Using RTC's in depth interview process and full staff of over 20 storytelling experts, clients' powerful messages are brought to the surface in their own words and eventually used to shape a full manuscript that is then packaged by the RTC team for distribution.

The majority of clients who work with RTC engage them for years and on multiple projects, demonstrating that the company's core values of brilliance, joy, honesty, momentum, and growth have proven to create an atmosphere where storytelling magic and personal transformation can occur.

NADJA BAER

Nadja has been a words-nerd all her life. She speaks English, German, Italian, and Spanish (with varying degrees of fluency), can teach Taekwondo classes in Korean, and is currently working on expanding her French vocabulary. Since receiving a Bachelor's degree in Creative Writing at the University of Minnesota, she has served as the office thesaurus, dictionary, translator, and spell-checker in every one of her day jobs. She wrote her first terrible novella at the age of eight, and is now focused on writing comics and novels for young adults. Her work can be seen for free in the online graphic novel, *Impure Blood* (www.impure bloodwebcomic.com), which is drawn by her soon-to-be husband. Other projects she has scripted for Round Table include *Everything's Okay* (Sept 2011) and *Delivering Happiness* (March 2012). Aside from a love of a good story with pretty pictures, they share a house, a cat, a turtle, and a belief that more people should embrace their inner nerd.

NATHAN LUETH

Nathan came into existence with a pencil in his hand, a feat that continues to confound obstetricians to this day. No one knows for sure when he started drawing or where his love of comics came from, but most experts agree that his professional career began after graduating from the Minneapolis College of Art and Design, as a caricaturist in the Mall of America. Soon he was freelance illustrating for the likes of Target, General Mills, and Stone Arch Books.

When not drawing comics for other people, Nathan draws his own super awesome fantasy webcomic, *Impure Blood* (www.impureblood-webcomic.com). He is proud to be a part of Writers of the Round Table, as he believes that comics should be for everyone, not just nerds (it should be noted that he may be trying to turn the general population into nerds). With Round Table he has also illustrated *Overachievement* by Dr. John Eliot (April 2011). He resides in St. Paul, Minnesota, with a cat, a turtle, and his imminent wife, Nadja, upon whom he performs his nerd conversion experiments.

THE UNITED STATES
CONSTITUTION
A Round Table Comic

CURRICULUM

COMMISSIONED BY MAUPIN HOUSE

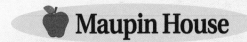

Round Table Companies worked in conjunction with educational publisher Maupin House and Author/Professor Dr. Katie Monnin to create a free curriculum guide for teachers and educators to use as a resource when utilizing the book in the classroom.

FOR YOUR FREE DIGITAL COPY PLEASE VISIT:
WWW.MAUPINHOUSE.COM/CONSTITUTIONCURRICULUM

FOR QUESTIONS ABOUT OUR EDUCATIONAL INITIATIVES PLEASE CONTACT:
DAVID COHEN (DAVID@ROUNDTABLECOMPANIES.COM)

CHECK OUT THESE
OTHER GREAT TITLES
FROM
ROUND TABLE COMICS...

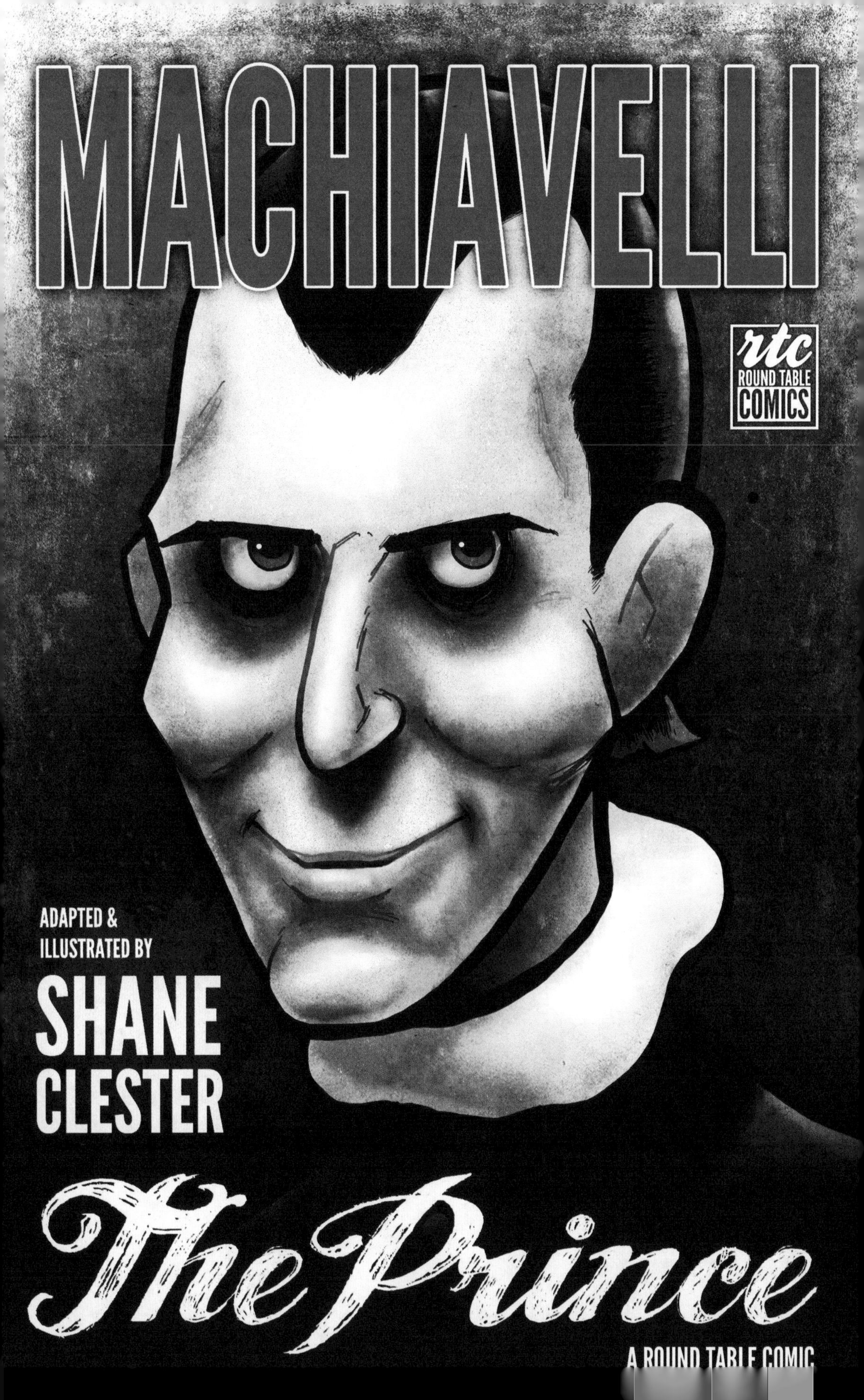
MACHIAVELLI
rtc
ROUND TABLE
COMICS
ADAPTED &
ILLUSTRATED BY
SHANE
CLESTER
The Prince
A ROUND TABLE COMIC

SmarterComics™

Based on the book *From the Barrio to the Board Room*

MI BARRIO

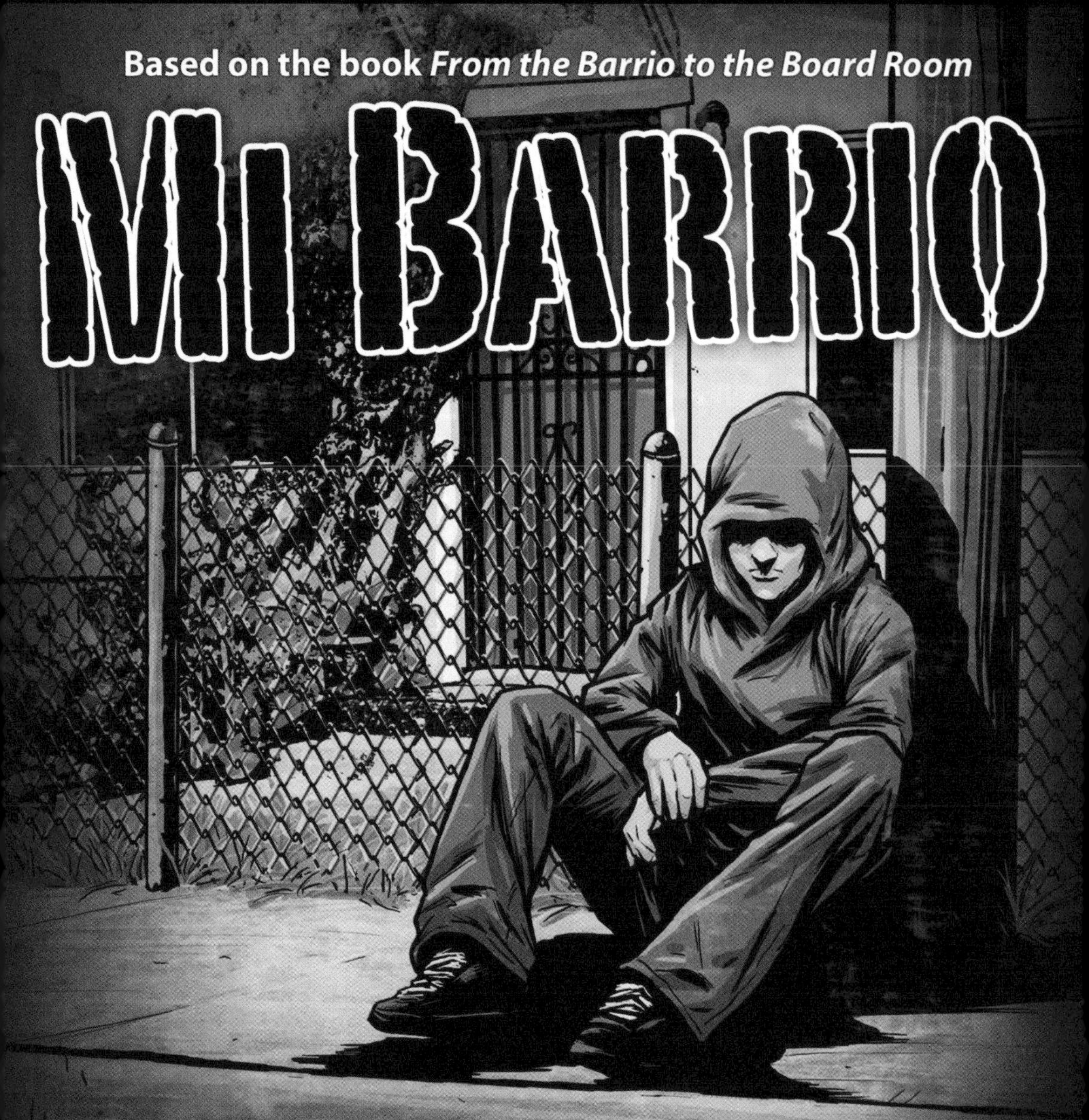

"DON'T LET WHERE YOU CAME FROM DICTATE WHO YOU ARE, BUT LET IT BE PART OF WHO YOU BECOME."

ROBERT RENTERIA

As told to **Corey Michael Blake**

Illustrated by **Shane Clester**

Free Curriculum Available

NOW A MOVEMENT!

DELIVERING happiness™

A PATH TO
PROFITS, PASSION, AND PURPOSE

TONY HSIEH
CEO, Zappos.com, Inc.

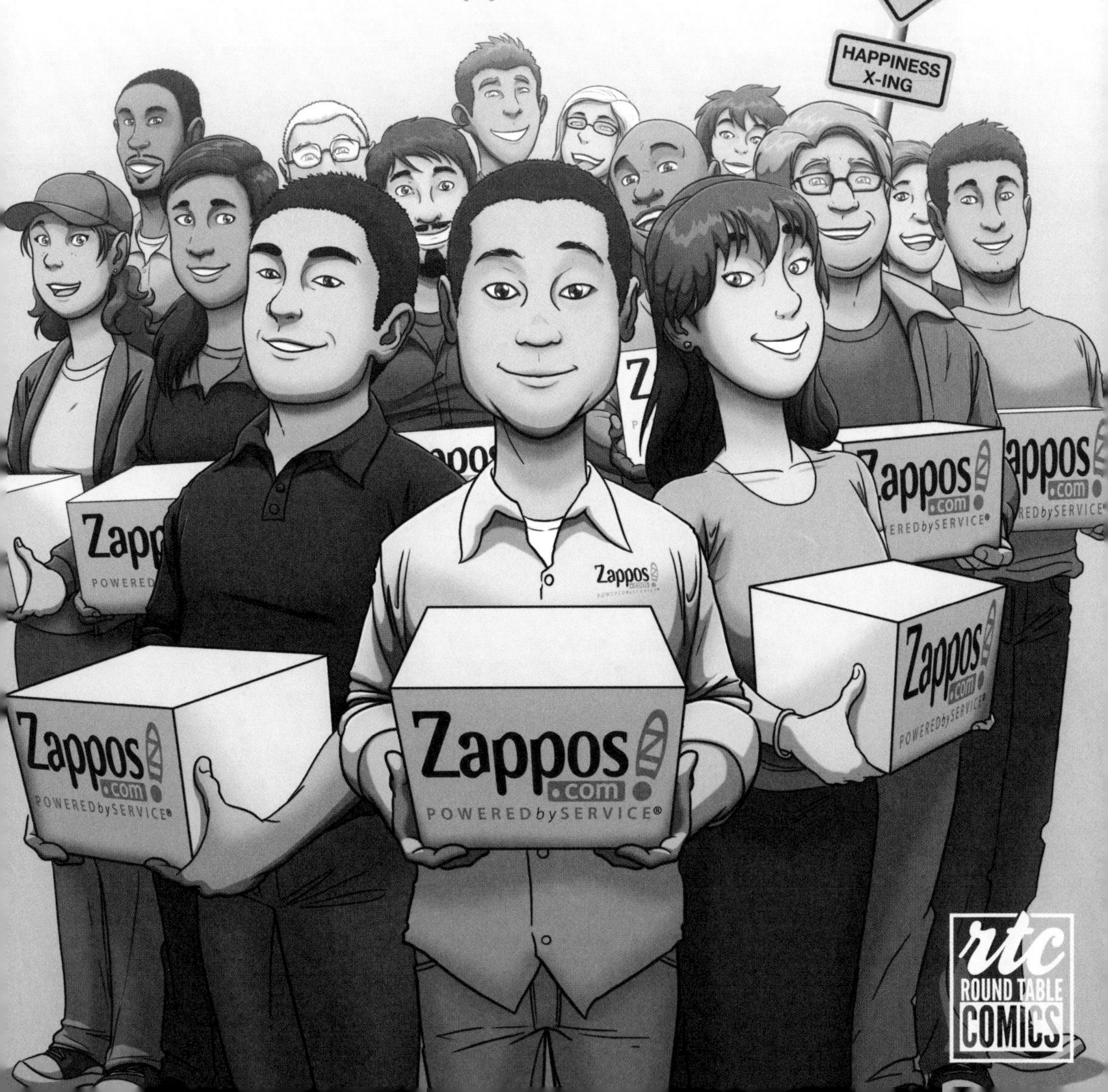

HAPPINESS X-ING
Zappos .com POWERED by SERVICE®
rtc ROUND TABLE COMICS

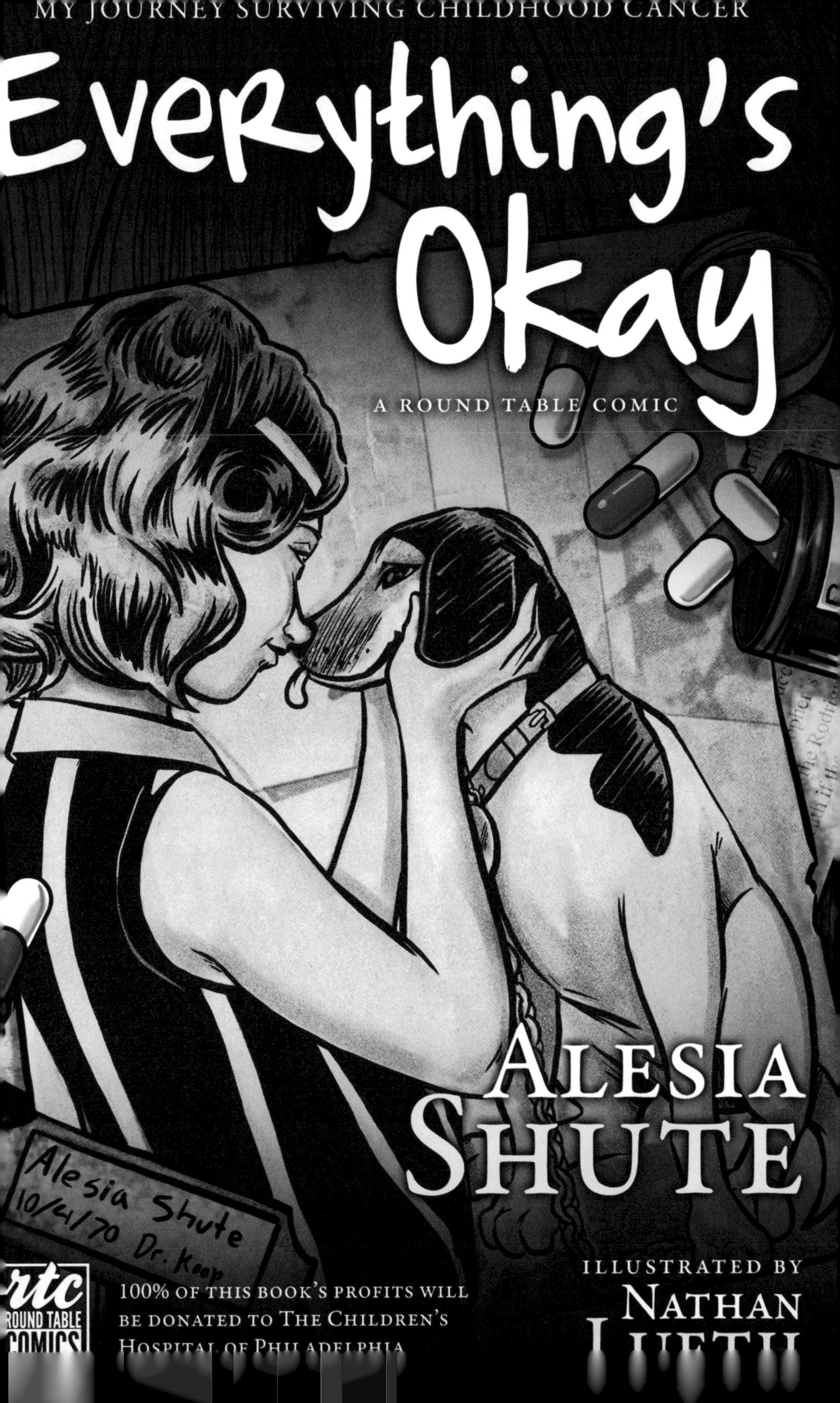
Alesia Shute
10/4/70 Dr. Koop

MY JOURNEY SURVIVING CHILDHOOD CANCER

Everything's Okay

A ROUND TABLE COMIC

ALESIA SHUTE

ILLUSTRATED BY

NATHAN

rtc ROUND TABLE COMICS

100% OF THIS BOOK'S PROFITS WILL BE DONATED TO THE CHILDREN'S HOSPITAL OF PHILADELPHIA

WWW.ROUNDTABLECOMPANIES.COM